Bob Blair has compiled thought-pro⌐
tered sermons based on the Gospel of
by insights from biblical scholarship or. ... .
practical applications reflecting mid-western perspectives and
sensibilities. This volume will serve as a valuable supplement
to a devotional reading of the gospels, and to Luke in partic-
ular.

Daniel A. Rodriguez, PhD,
Professor of Religion,
Pepperdine University

Robert Blair employs simple, familiar metaphors to explain
how all events and encounters with Jesus in the New Tes-
tament have relevance to contemporary life and attitudes.
Viewed as a manual, the book is scholarly documented, and if
seen as a guide book, it is relationally practical for modern life.
It will also help teachers to rediscover Luke's stories on the life
and teachings of Jesus Christ. The book is highly recommend-
ed, not only for religious practitioners, but for scholars alike.

Dr. Eno Otoyo, Pioneer Educator with the
Los Angeles Unified School System

Some years ago I was privileged to read The Great Omis-
sion, *with author Bob Blair's reflections on Christians' strug-*
gles in relating to governments and cultures, with the result
that often the *fundamental mission of the church is neglected.*
Bob amplifies this theme in Luke Alive: 26 Sermons on the
Gospel of Luke, *focusing on Jesus' pointed and masterful*
challenges to the culture of his own day. Many of these lessons
are puzzling to our modern world, and the passages are often
neglected in today's preaching and teaching. This book takes a
fresh look at these texts, and brings them home with illustra-
tions from Bob's life and work and wisdom in the Lord. It will
enlighten your mind, and lift your heart.

Larry Walker
Oxford, Mississippi

ROBERT BLAIR

VOLUME 1

13 SERMONS ON THE GOSPEL OF LUKE

CSS Publishing Company, Inc.
Lima, Ohio

LUKE ALIVE VOLUME 1
13 SERMONS BASED ON THE GOSPEL OF LUKE

FIRST EDITION
Copyright © 2018
by CSS Publishing Co., Inc.

Published by CSS Publishing Company, Inc., Lima, Ohio 45807. All rights re-
served. No part of this publication may be reproduced in any manner whatsoever
without the prior permission of the publisher, except in the case of brief quota-
tions embodied in critical articles and reviews. Inquiries should be addressed to:
CSS Publishing Company, Inc., Permissions Department, 5450 N. Dixie Highway, Lima, Ohio 45807.

Library of Congress Cataloging-in-Publication Data

Names: Blair, Robert, 1936- author.
Title: Luke alive : 13 sermons based on the gospel of Luke / by Robert Blair.
Description: First edition. | Lima : CSS Publishing Company, Inc., 2019. |
   Includes bibliographical references and index.
Identifiers: LCCN 2018047969 (print) | LCCN 2018054546 (ebook) | ISBN
   9780788028960 (eBook) | ISBN 9780788028953 (vol. 1 : pbk. : alk. paper)
Subjects: LCSH: Bible. Luke--Sermons.
Classification: LCC BS2595.54 (ebook) | LCC BS2595.54 B53 2019 (print) |
DDC
   252--dc23

For more information about CSS Publishing Company resources, visit our web-
site at www.csspub.com, email us at csr@csspub.com, or call (800) 241-4056.

e-book:
ISBN-13: 978-0-7880-2896-0
ISBN-10: 0-7880-2896-0

ISBN-13: 978-0-7880-2895-3
ISBN-10: 0-7880-2895-2

PRINTED IN USA

Contents

3

I thank God for the opportunity that David Runk and CSS Publishing Company have provided me to share these sermons. The Lord blessed me with a patient, devoted, loving wife (Norma) and a supportive, godly family.

Church families in Northwest Iowa, especially Cleghorn and Kingsley, as well as The Hollywood Church of Christ have given us extraordinary encouragement.

I am grateful to Larry Walker, to Dr. Eno Otoyo, to Daniel A. Rodriguez, PhD, Professor of Religion, Pepperdine University, and to my brother, Gary Blair. Each one has been very helpful. CSS Project Coordinator Karyl Corson has been very professional and accommodating.

God is good.

His wisdom is profound.

His love is boundless.

1
Luke 1:26-38

The Angel's Nazareth Mission

In the sixth month, God sent the angel Gabriel to Nazareth, a town in Galilee, to a virgin pledged to be married to a man named Joseph, a descendant of David. The virgin's name was Mary.

The angel went to her and said, "Greetings, you who are highly favored! The Lord is with you."

Mary was greatly troubled at his words and wondered what kind of greeting this might be.

But the angel said to her, "Do not be afraid, Mary, you have found favor with God. You will be with child and give birth to a son, and you are to give him the name Jesus. He will be great and will be called the Son of the Most High. The Lord God will give him the throne of his father David, and he will reign over the house of Jacob forever; his kingdom will never end."

"How will this be," Mary asked the angel, "since I am a virgin?"

The angel answered, "The Holy Spirit will come upon you, and the power of the Most High will overshadow you. So the holy one to be born will be called the Son of God. Even Elizabeth your relative is going to have a child in her old age, and she who was said to be barren is in her sixth month. For nothing is impossible with God."

"I am the Lord's servant," Mary answered. "May it be to me as you have said." Then the angel left her. (NIV)

Do you feel as though God favors you? Do you feel that he is on your side? Do you feel he is always with you?

We humans have a need for approval. My wife bought an electric toothbrush. That new brush gives us a digital readout of the duration we have brushed our teeth. If we brush our teeth at least two minutes, a little smiley-face appears. It does not appear at 1:59. We must get fully to two minutes. I make sure I get all the way there. One more second makes little difference to the cleanliness of my teeth. It is silly but I keep brushing all the way to two full minutes because I love the sense of approval I feel when I see that happy face.

Suppose tonight a messenger from God appeared to you and said: "Good evening. You have won God's favor. He's with you." Would it help you to know that God approves of you? That he is on your side? That he smiles with approval?

You may be thinking, "This is not going to happen. How many "virgin Marys" can there be?" You are right about that part. It will not happen again. No other savior is coming. Jesus' birth won't be repeated. The Son of God came to our planet, lived perfectly, died, was buried, and was raised to life. He appeared once for all. That part is clear. The next time everyone sees Jesus, it will be Judgment Day. But does that mean God no longer looks favorably on people as he did with Mary?

Here is our theme today. God still gives people something extraordinary, special, and winsome. Do you know how to get that extra? To win God's favor? For sure Mary was qualified in certain ways that we shall never achieve. None of us meets the criteria in ways she did. First, Mary was a Jewish virgin. She was engaged at the time, but not married. Those facts disqualify most of us. Especially, we guys do not have a chance, do we? We live in a different time, and most of us lack biological and ethnic qualifications.

Those facts eliminate us from giving birth to the savior. But we can still win God's favor; even today.

We shall see how we can do that. But first a word about angels. Folks today are fixated on angels. So much is written and said about angels, it is hard to separate myth from fact. Folks also speculate about extraterrestrial beings. Do they exist? Is there life out there somewhere? The question motivates space exploration. Scientists send signals into space hoping some beings will respond. They look for signs of life on Mars. They hope that every new planet they discover will lead them to the answer. Is there life out there somewhere?

For centuries the Bible has informed us that life is not confined to this planet. Other forms of life do appear in our universe. Some are called "angels." Some are called "cherubim." Some are called "seraphim." We cannot spend much time talking about cherubim and seraphim today. They are extraterrestrial and different. Both cherubim and seraphim have wings. Seraphim resemble some spiders in one way. They have lots of eyes. Unlike spiders, however, they tend to be fiery. Our main concern today, though, is angels.

Here are a few basics about angels. The word angel means "messenger." Imagine powerful rulers, who keep spokespeople and couriers nearby. Some they send with important messages to different places and people. Presidents use diplomats to explain and get the word out. At times the Lord uses angels to do that. He sent the angel Gabriel to Mary.

We first read about Gabriel in the Old Testament book of Daniel. Gabriel encouraged Daniel. That is what God's angels often do — inform and encourage people. They carry upbeat messages from God. [1] God

1   God also sent his heavenly agents to warn human beings (see Genesis 18ff.).

used these agents because our nature is different from his. God's greatness is everywhere throughout the universe, but we are confined to a few cubic feet of space. At times then, God sends representatives in human likeness to communicate with us. These couriers from God convey important information to us on this little planet.

In Genesis 18, Abraham entertained three *"men."* He and his wife Sarah killed a fatted calf, baked bread, fed the three men, and helped them wash their feet. They did not know that the three were not ordinary men — not until the trio told Abraham their mission. They were angels; one of them, the angel of the Lord. The angels Gabriel and Michael looked like men.

Here is where we separate myth from fact. No angel in the Bible had wings.[2] The facts about angels are: They appeared in human form. They appeared as males. Most angels are messengers of God, but some are agents of Satan.

So the angel Gabriel, who spoke to Daniel about 600 years prior, came to Mary and said. "Greetings, you who are highly favored!"

Is it possible to win God's favor now? Some of my acquaintances keep waiting for a sign from God that he has chosen them. They hope that God will send one of his messengers to talk with them. They want the Lord to tell them how special they are.

Is it still possible to win God's favor? If so, how can we make it happen? Mary had more than just biological and family connections going for her. So did the other people that God gave special favor.

---

2   The New Testament word for angel is ὁ ἄγγελος, pronounced ángelos; the "ὁ" (Greek omicron) tells us that the word ὁ ἄγγελος is masculine. Feminine words are preceded by another Greek vowel, η=English long A

Let's quickly look at a few characteristics that help bring God's approval. I get the feeling that Mary was not just sitting around tweeting her friends and waiting for text messages. Biblical examples show that God favors active people. Jewish rabbis would have said that the only time you want to hire a lazy man is when you need to send for the angel of death.

God chose Rebekah to be the mother of Jacob (Israel). Rebekah qualified because she readily volunteered to do really hard work (see Genesis 24). It is sweaty labor to water a bunch of camels. "Ships of the desert" can guzzle several gallons at a time. Rebekah drew water from a well, carried it in a clay jar, and poured it into a trough or container for the whole caravan.

When God chose Elisha, the future prophet was supervising eleven other guys while they plowed. Elisha tilled along with them but not in a huge John Deere or Case International with GPS, air conditioning, and Dolby sound. He cultivated using two oxen yoked together and kept his plow steady. If we want God's favor, we cannot be sitting on our duffs. He uses busy people.

Second, God chooses upbeat people. Mary was not perfect. But you can tell from Mary's response, that she was cheery and positive.

I have spent too much of my life focusing on the faults of other people. I have told long tales of woe about things going wrong and other people's flaws — blaming them. If you find me going there, I hope you will kick me in the pants. Remind me to get out of that mode.

One last thing about winning God's favor. God has already favored us (chosen us) in Christ. "By grace we are saved through faith." The cross is God's sign that he has chosen-favored us and all who accept him.

The word for angel is *angelos* (Greek – ἄγγελος). That word *angelos* (ἄγγελος) is the main stem of another word *euangelion* (εὐαγγέλιον), which means "message of good news" (the gospel), and *euangelistās* (εὐαγγελιστής), an evangelist or preacher of good news.

The good news is: God is on our side. As Paul wrote in Romans 8:31, *"If God is for us, who can be against us?"*

A few weeks ago I complained to several people about not getting good racquetball partners when I play doubles. If you do not have a capable partner, it is hard to win. The partners who had to play with me likely made the same complaint. They were probably stuck with a worse teammate.

If we accept God's good news in Christ we have the most powerful life-force in the universe (God) as our partner — *"Who can be against us?"*

When we align ourselves with God, nothing can defeat us. But we must follow him and obey him; we do not enjoy his favor when we don't act according to his word.

Repent of your pride .

Accept Christ.

Partner with God.

You cannot lose. You will enjoy God's favor throughout eternity.

God bless you!

2

Luke 4:14-21

Will You Enjoy The Year Of The Lord's Favor?

Jesus returned to Galilee in the power of the Spirit, and news about him spread through the whole countryside. He taught in their synagogues, and everyone praised him.

He went to Nazareth, where he had been brought up, and on the Sabbath day he went into the synagogue, as was his custom. And he stood up to read.

The scroll of the prophet Isaiah was handed to him. Unrolling it, he found the place where it is written: "The Spirit of the Lord is on me, because he has anointed me to preach good news to the poor. He has sent me to proclaim freedom for the prisoners and recovery of sight for the blind, to release the oppressed, to proclaim the year of the Lord's favor." (NIV)

Thesis: Over the course of our lives, the Lord gives us opportunities to obey him. Wise folks grab them every chance they get.

Our text today deals with time and opportunity. We know the limitations of time. Many of us battle the clock every day. But opportunities are also limited. Recall the old maxim, "Opportunity knocks only once"? An old, Bulgarian proverb advises, "Seize opportunity by the beard, for it is bald behind."

Have you gone back to your home town after being gone for a while? Did you get the reception that you expected? I went to high school in Milwaukie, Oregon, just south of Portland. After a few years, life changed a lot for me. During that interim, I spent two years in college, Norma and I were married, and I had decided to become a minister.

One evening I went to the Dairy Queen in downtown Milwaukie. I hung out a lot there during high school. Several of my former classmates gathered in the parking lot that evening and were talking about old times. When they asked me what I had been doing, I told them about my plans for ministry. One of them looked genuinely shocked and said, "You, Bob, a minister?" Why they were incredulous, you will have to guess.

We do not know how long Jesus had been away from his hometown, Nazareth. It could have been years; it might have been only a few months, but at age thirty he began his ministry. He had John the Baptist baptize him, and then Jesus spent time in the wilderness being tested by the devil.

Jesus traveled back north to the area of Galilee. He soon gained fame as a miracle-worker and synagogue teacher. He became a cause célèbre. People everywhere talked about him. Then Jesus went home and attended the synagogue worship service. That in itself tells us something about his faithfulness at worship. Many churches use pre-assigned or lectionary readings from the Old Testament, the Psalms, the Gospels, and the balance of the New Testament each Sunday. Jewish services began with a recitation of the Shema (Deuteronomy 6:4-9 NIV). It begins, "Hear, O Israel: The LORD our God, the LORD is one. Love the LORD your God with all your heart and with all your soul and with all your strength."

They recited it as a prayer and then followed eighteen benedictions. After that came readings from the law (the first five books of the Old Testament or Pentateuch). After the readings of the law they read from the prophets. At times visiting rabbis were invited to read from the prophets. The visitors might have been free to choose their own readings and then comment on them. Possibly when Jesus read from Isaiah 61 that morning, it was the assigned (lectionary) reading for that particular sabbath.

The Jews then did not keep the Bible in book form. The Old Testament was on hand-written scrolls. They kept those treasured writings in a portable cabinet called an arc. They placed the arc immediately behind the speaking area. Speakers spoke from an elevated platform called a bema. Synagogue leaders sat in the chief seats that faced the congregation. Men and women sat separately. A custodian handed Jesus the Isaiah scroll.

At that time, the Bible had no chapter and verse divisions. There was hardly any punctuation. It probably took Jesus a few moments to unroll the Isaiah scroll to the place now designated as chapter 61. These facts tell me that Jesus knew the book of Isaiah very well. About 700 years earlier, the prophet Isaiah wrote the passage Jesus chose.

Jesus' scripture selection speaks of the Christ. Jesus let the hometown folks know that this 700-year-old prophecy was being fulfilled right before their eyes — he was God's anointed, the Messiah. The Bible views history as flowing according to God's plan. In Jesus, God was bringing a new era, a time of his favor.

When my parents first moved to Oregon we lived in a backward suburb called Oak Grove. About a mile west of where we lived, Oak Grove Boulevard descended down a long hill to the banks of the Willamette River, a tributary of the Columbia. At Oak Grove the Willamette is wider than the Missouri River in Sioux City and flows much slower. As a kid I watched tug boats move log rafts down the river. We often saw sternwheelers carrying cargo between Oregon City and Portland.

To a Kansas kid who had seen mostly muddy creeks and streams, the Willamette River seemed an awesome thing. It silently flowed, a habitat for fish and game, at the same time, conveying goods and debris. The tug boats, log rafts, and sternwheelers I saw as a kid are long gone. Pleasure craft and fishing boats now replace them. In a few years they will give way to more modern craft.

The flow of history is like that. It carries some of us along for a short ride. Then we give way to "newer" folks and we shall permanently leave the river. What Jesus read that day in the synagogue concerns the flow of time and the opportunity it gives each of us.

My explanation requires some contemporary history. I was watching a Kansas-Missouri basketball game one evening. Kansas was supposed to easily defeat Missouri, but Missouri played amazingly well and it looked like they might defeat the highly favored Jayhawks. During the last ten minutes of the game, a Kansas freshman suddenly came alive, hit several three-point-shots and made some defensive moves that changed the game. The young man was from an eastern city and knew nothing of the Kansas-Missouri border rivalry that goes back to Civil War times. Bill Self, the Kansas coach, talked with his players, explaining to this young freshman how much the game meant. The freshman came out playing with the passion of Carrie Nation. In case you have forgotten, Carrie Nation was a woman who, after her husband died of alcoholism, tore up Kansas saloons with a hatchet. The freshman basketball player said that he just needed a little history lesson.

Let's have a similar history lesson now. When the Lord gave the promised land to Israel, his promise was conditional. He gave property to all of them. In fact he gave every family of each tribe a piece of land. But he required something of them. They were to:

Honor God with all their heart, soul, and mind.
Keep the law of Moses.
Treat one another well.
Teach their children respect for the law.

A few of the laws the Lord gave might seem a little strange to us. First, when he gave families land, he intended that the land remain with that family and its descendants forever. It was never to leave that family's permanent possession. Boundary markers were set up. Those who moved them faced grave penalties. According to the law of Moses, farm land could not be bought and sold. At the most, one could get a 49-year lease because every fiftieth year, the land was supposed to revert to the original owner. The Lord made that arrangement so no Israelite family would ever be destitute.

Recent news reports told of a poor guy who won several hundred million dollars in a lottery a few years prior. Now he is bankrupt. "How could that happen?" you ask. Certain people are simply not good money managers. In Old Testament times, some people got so far in debt that they sold their own lives. They became slaves. Built into the law of Moses was the requirement that every fiftieth year, slaves had to be freed and all land reverted to the original owners or their heirs. That was the year of Jubilee. To my knowledge, no Israelite generation ever celebrated a Jubilee.

People forgot God's laws; they became corrupt, greedy, and selfish. They never observed the freedom and joy that Jubilee would have brought them. Many people were forced to become bondservants. Other slaves got that way because their country lost wars.

Some became slaves of their own doing. They had turned their lives over to alcohol, pornography, gambling, bitterness, anger, and the like. In case you are wondering, yes pornography was rampant then, too. Most folks were miserable and in disarray.

Jesus' synagogue reading that day gave hope to all of us who mess up. He brought "the year of the Lord's favor." God does not restrict his favor to a single year, however. Chronological time is not the issue here, anyhow. We are talking about opportunities Jesus gives us to correct our lives. When they mess up, many want someone to pick them up out of their misery and give them a nice warm fuzzy, or they want the Lord to send them bells and whistles and tell them that everything is okay. Some expect to hear a small voice tell them that they are all right.

Jesus expects us to repent and change our ways. He demands that we believe that he (Jesus) is the only Son of God. Acts 10:34 (NIV) makes that clear: *"Then Peter began to speak: 'I now realize how true it is that God does not show favoritism but accepts men from every nation who fear him and do what is right.'"*

Have you changed your lifestyle? Given up adultery? Drunkenness? Hate? Anger? Jesus said, *"The Spirit of the Lord is on me, because he has anointed me to preach good news to the poor. He has sent me to proclaim freedom for the prisoners and recovery of sight for the blind, to release the oppressed, to proclaim the year of the Lord's favor."* Jesus brought the opportunity for the Lord's favor. But we must change our lives and believe him in order to enjoy it. But can that still happen today?

Let me share a story of the gospel's power. A recent article in *Christianity Today* told of a prison ministry known as *InnerChange*. A picture showed workers baptizing by immersion a 44-year-old man in a Texas prison. His arms and the backs of his hands were covered with tattoos. The brief caption authenticated the gospel's power to effect change even in hardened people.

Prison populations have been exploding. At year-end in 1980, there were 329,821 prisoners under the supervision of state and federal correctional authorities. By 2004, the figure had more than quadrupled to 1,496,629. "It has certainly been a growing mission field," says Prison Fellowship President Mark Earley.

Earnest Myers, 44, was baptized by members of Prison Fellowship's *InnerChange* Freedom Initiative. Myers was convicted of committing crimes in six states and has spent much of his life in prison. *InnerChange* tries to reduce recidivism. Currently, two-thirds of the 600,000 prisoners released each year will be re-arrested within three years. For those who complete the *InnerChange* program, which operates inside prisons, the re-arrest rate is 17%.[3] Jesus has brought his time of favor to us. He is the world's only hope.

3   *Christianity Today*, October 2006, p — 62

A sweet, elderly lady named Nora attended church in Hollywood. Nora and her daughter lived in an apartment not far from the Hollywood Freeway. She faithfully attended services; her daughter did not. The daughter made a comfortable living writing for magazines that featured stories about Hollywood movie stars. She never attended services and never showed interest in serving Jesus. Many encouraged her to alter her life. She refused.

Upon Nora's death, the daughter changed her attitude and began serving the Lord. Though we were delighted that she accepted Jesus, it seemed sad that she never did so sooner. Her mother would have known the joy of seeing her daughter in the Lord. The daughter had many opportunities. She never took them.

The Lord extends you an opportunity at this moment to accept him and change your life. As Paul made clear: (2 Corinthians 6:2 NIV) *"For he says, "In the time of my favor I heard you, and in the day of salvation I helped you." I tell you, now is the time of God's favor, now is the day of salvation."*

I pray that you will not miss this opportunity to enjoy his favor and his salvation. We never know when we might be removed from our place in the flow of time.

God bless you!

3
Luke 6:1-11

Does Sunday Equal The Sabbath?

One Sabbath Jesus was going through the grain fields, and his disciples began to pick some heads of grain, rub them in their hands and eat the kernels. Some of the Pharisees asked, "Why are you doing what is unlawful on the Sabbath?

Jesus answered them, "Have you never read what David did when he and his companions were hungry? He entered the house of God, and taking the consecrated bread, he ate what is lawful only for priests to eat. And he also gave some to his companions." Then Jesus said to them, "The Son of Man is Lord of the Sabbath."

On another Sabbath he went into the synagogue and was teaching, and a man was there whose right hand was shriveled. The Pharisees and the teachers of the law were looking for a reason to accuse Jesus, so they watched him closely to see if he would heal on the Sabbath. But Jesus knew what they were thinking and said to the man with the shriveled hand, "Get up and stand in front of everyone." So he got up and stood there.

Then Jesus said to them, "I ask you, which is lawful on the Sabbath: to do good or to do evil, to save life or to destroy it?"

He looked around at them all, and then said to the man, "Stretch out your hand." He did so, and his hand was completely restored. But they were furious and began to discuss with one another what they might do to Jesus. (NIV)

My wife does not like me to bet with her money. And I do not like to bet with *my* money. That means that all bets are off today. So, how about a wager? I am kidding, of course, but if my wife put all of her money on the line, she could not lose if I made the following wager: I am betting that none of you has ever lost sleep or spent one anxious thought about the question in today's sermon title.

Who cares and what does it matter whether Sunday equals the sabbath? Whether Sunday equals the sabbath is hardly the world's most pressing issue. If you polled ten thousand people, scant numbers would rank it in their top ten thousand most important questions. But, what if you found that knowing the answer to the question would save you time and make life simpler for you? Would you be interested? As you know, preachers can be terrible time-wasters. I hate to admit it, but you know it is true.

Preachers fritter almost as much of your time as politicians. Not only do they misuse your time, both groups like to string words together that sound impressive, but actually mislead you. "In the 1970s, the White House announced that an earlier statement made by the administration should now be considered. 'no longer operative.' How do you translate: 'no longer operative'? Literal translation: It was a lie."[4]

When preachers and politicians say things in splendid sounding words, it usually means one of two things:

1) It could mean that they do not know what they are talking about.

2) It could mean that they are purposely trying to hide the real meaning from you.

Both groups mix intricate laws with highbrow words. They make things extra complicated. God's

4 *Success with Words,* Reader's Digest

words are usually simple and clear. Ministers, politicians, and professors artfully use vague, complex, muddled language to confuse you.

Recently news-people showed at least five different videos of a Massachusetts Institute of Technology professor. The academic was the chief advisor for one of the most significant pieces of legislation ever passed by the US Congress. One video showed him speaking at an academic conference. The professor described American voters as too stupid to understand. His elite audience laughed in agreement.

It probably does not shock you that religious leaders concluded the same thing about ordinary people in Jesus' time. Those elites despised Jesus because he exposed the pretense and hypocrisy of the leaders. Those chiefs hid behind complicated laws. Jesus simplified things.

John's gospel tells us the leaders sent some temple guards to arrest Jesus. The enforcement officers went to take him into custody. But after they met Jesus and he talked with them, they believed Jesus was who he said he was. The guards returned without him.

"Why didn't you bring him in? the leaders demanded. "He says such wonderful things!" ... "We've never heard anything like it," the guards replied. "So you also have been led astray?" the Pharisees mocked. Is there a single one of us Jewish rulers or Pharisees" they said "who believes he is the Messiah? These stupid crowds do, yes; but what do they know about it?" (Living Bible, John 7: 45-49).

It should not amaze you that a twenty-first- century MIT professor and first-century professors from Jerusalem "University" had contempt for ordinary people. The problem is not the stupidity of people. It is pretense, pride, and hypocrisy of politicians, preachers, and professors. Let's clear some confusion that leaders have created about the Bible and its laws. For instance human labeling within the Bible often creates misunderstandings.

Tables of Content in English Bibles read *Old Testament* and *New Testament*. "Testament" is an old French word for will.[5] Most of us have a few pages of "legalese" (high-sounding words) tucked away in a safe deposit box, in a dresser under our jammies, or in a cabinet. It is our "last will and testament."

On rare occasions, Bible writers used the term testament to refer to a will. The Bible word "testament" usually denotes an agreement or a contract.[6] Covenants are made between two parties. For example, God made covenants with Noah (Genesis 6:18 & 9:8-17), Abraham (Genesis 12:1-3 & Galatians 3:15-25), and David.[7] They are still in effect.

What Christians call the Old Testament is what Jewish people call their *holy scriptures*. The *holy scriptures* includes the same 39 books as in Christian Old Testaments. Jewish people merely place the books in a different order.[8] To summarize, "testament" in the Bible usually refers to an agreement between two parties; often between God and certain people.

5   It harks back to the Norman invasion of England. The elite people spoke French; only common folks spoke English. Source: *Creative Writing*, Kathryn Lindskoog, p. 106

6   Hebrews 9:16 ff. is a notable exception, where the writer applies it to the new covenant put into effect by the blood of Jesus. It did not come into force until Jesus died (shed his blood). He also remarks that the blood of animals served in a proxy way to put the Mosaic covenant into place.

7   In Galatians Paul explained that God's covenant with Abraham to bless all people through his seed (Christ) is still in effect. It blesses those of all nations who have faith in Christ. Moses' Law came 430 years after the Abrahamic covenant. The covenant with Israel (including the Ten Commandments) served only as a tutor or was "put in charge to lead us to Christ that we might be justified by faith. Now that faith has come, we are no longer under the supervision of the law," (Galatians 3:24, 25 & see Galatians 4).

8   They follow the order Jesus mentioned in Luke 24:44.

But we must ask, "Is it appropriate to put the label 'old' on this agreement (testament)?" I hear Christian people say "We don't go by the old Bible anymore." Of course right now, many folks do not go by any part of the Bible. Trying to decide which is worse is like deciding whether it is a bigger mistake to misread a map or to not use a map at all.

The label "old" for the first part of the Bible clearly misleads people. Some of you may be wine connoisseurs. I would not know chardonnay if they threw me into a barrel of it. I might be full of it but I still could not distinguish it from port. Suppose someone sent me to a wine cellar to select a bottle of wine for dinner. I might select on the basis of the cleanest or neatest looking bottle, not the oldest. I might also return and tell the host that I found some old dusty bottles down there so I just poured them out.

Tossing out the Old Testament or neglecting it, thinking it is all outdated, would be a worse mistake. It contains important agreements and vital laws that still apply to us. What would I be tossing? For one, I would be neglecting the most simple, eloquent description of how our universe started that was ever written.

The scientists who recently put a "lander" on that icy comet did an amazing feat. But in my opinion, the pride scientists and technicians took in that and in similar accomplishments is a little like this: Suppose you build an elaborate tree house for some young children. You purposely build it so that it is several feet off the ground — not easily accessible. It will take considerable time and effort for the kids to climb and gain entrance to the house. After much time and struggle, the kids finally get there. But instead of appreciating your design, craftsmanship, and unselfishness in providing it, they only brag and high-five themselves on getting to the tree house.

If an object such as that recent comet is so complex and distant that it takes the brilliant minds of a thousand human beings to get the lander to it, how did it and other space objects come to be in the first place without a grand designer? This writing that some call "old" speaks simply but powerfully of origins — *"In the beginning, God created ..."* That phrase is only three words in the original language. Not many words later, Genesis eloquently described how God made men and women and shortly after, Genesis defined marriage.

Some religious leaders arrived to test Jesus on the subject of divorce (Matthew 19). The two most esteemed experts of Jesus' time did not agree on what provided legal grounds for divorce. The cause has to be grave, insisted one. If your wife burns your breakfast pita bread, you can "get rid of" her, said the other. So some important leaders came to ask Jesus his opinion: *"'is it lawful for a man to divorce his wife for any and every reason?'" 'Haven't you read,' he replied, 'that at the beginning the creator made them male and female and said, '"For this reason a man will leave his father and mother and be united to his wife, and the two will become one flesh?" 'So they are no longer two, but one. Therefore what God has joined together, let man not separate'"(3b-6).* [9]

God created us male and female; a guy leaves his dad and mom; he is united to his wife and the two become one flesh. That means that I would divorce my wife with the same reluctance that I would agree to have my leg amputated. This is one of those agreements-contracts-covenants found in what is now called

9   Jesus was here quoting from Genesis 1:27 and 2:24

the Old Testament. Malachi the prophet (2:14) refers to *"your partner, the wife of your marriage covenant."* Husband and wife are one flesh.

What we call the Old Testament contains several agreements just like the marriage covenant. Some of the Old Testament agreements still apply to you and me. Jesus taught that the marriage covenant God created in the beginning has not changed and will not change. Many religious teachers fail to see that. Jesus clearly taught in Matthew 19 that nothing will alter the original Genesis marriage contract. What preachers, politicians, the courts, Hollywood stars, and virtually all major media people say means nothing. From the beginning Jesus said, marriage is between a man and a woman, and we divorce with the same eagerness that we would look forward to an amputation.

Genesis nine contains another principle that God never cancelled. The label "Old Testament" misleads people, right? We would not pour out all the aged wine just because the bottles are dusty. So what Old Testament agreements apply and which ones do not apply? Just like you would read labels in the wine cellar, we read labels on covenants. Exodus 20 serves as a good example. Here is how Exodus 20 begins: *"And God spoke all these words: 'I am the Lord your God, who brought you out of Egypt, out of the land of slavery.' 'You shall have no other gods before you.'"* The other nine commandments follow.

God gave the Ten Commandments to Israel when they first left Egypt. You and I did not come out of slavery in Egypt and I doubt any of our ancestors did. The ancestors of some current Jewish people came out of Egypt. But Jesus fulfilled all the law's obligations for even Jews: In Colossians chapter two, the former Jewish rabbi Paul, wrote: God made you alive with Christ. *"He forgave us all our sins, having cancelled the written code with its regulations, that was against us and that stood opposed to us; he took it away nailing it to the cross,"* (vv. 13-14).What did Paul mean: *"regulations … opposed to us and stood against us"?* Let's look at one instance.

One of the Ten Commandments is verse eight of Exodus 20: *"Remember the sabbath day by keeping it holy."* That law required rest on the seventh day, the sabbath; *"Do no work."* Just as the two esteemed sages argued about divorce law, so rabbis could not agree on what it was legal to do on the sabbath. An example of definition is found in the ancient Mishnah, Shabbath 20. 5.

Two thousand years ago, you could not buy a bed on which you could adjust the firmness or purchase a mattress that would assure you beautiful rest. Most people arranged straw and slept on it. Perhaps this happens to you: I often awaken at night and rearrange my pillow. It tends to clump and I raise my head so I can straighten the pillow. Suppose a Jew were sleeping on straw and the straw felt uncomfortably lumpy. If that happened on sabbath night, the Jew might have a problem. According to most rabbis, on the sabbath night, Jews could not use their hands to rearrange the straw. They could, however, shift it (the straw) with their bodies. In their judgment, using one's hand to move the straw was work. Scooting straw with one's body was not work. Compare the amount of energy expended using your hand with what it would take to move the straw with your whole body. You wonder: What were those guys thinking?

Ancient rabbis made thousands of rules like that. They bound other people with their decisions. Many so-called Christian leaders do the same. Religious leaders resemble politicians; they love to make laws for other people to obey. God designed the sabbath to give people healthful rest and to provide time and opportunity to honor him. Yet how could they get any rest or honor God when they had to worry about violating so many man-made rules?

Going back to our Luke 6 text, I have walked through wheat fields and done exactly what the apostles did. You break off heads of grain, rub them between the palms of your hands and pop the wheat grains into your mouth. The result of your work is not as tasty as pita bread or the cinnamon rolls some of you bake. It is simple and it is a tasty chew if you are hungry. It takes less work than some of the ordinary sabbath procedures. The leaders loved to control people. When Jesus refused to obey all of their man-made commandments, it upset the men in charge. It is evident where their hearts were.

Consider what happened when Jesus called the man forward at the synagogue whose hand was withered. Jesus healed him by merely speaking to him. He did much less work than trying to rearrange straw using the "body" method. Still, it enraged the leaders. Does the sabbath law apply to us? No and neither does any of the Ten Commandments. They were part of a set of laws given to Israel. Not to us.

Recall Exodus 20 and Galatians 3, 4? No one should try to apply the Ten Commandments to you, unless you are old enough to have come out of Egyptian slavery with Moses. So how do we know what to do? How are we to live? We use the contract Jeremiah the prophet (chapter 31) spoke of, a new covenant that would be written on hearts and minds of people.

The new covenant is not a set of laws; it is a relationship with God that Jesus lived and made possible. It means:

1) We put God first and thank him every day.

2) Remember that Jesus paid for your mistakes on the cross and he overcame death and you can, too, by trusting him? Jesus returned from his death on the first day of the week, not the seventh. That is why we gather especially on that first day of the week to honor his sacrifice and to celebrate his victory over death.

3) Love everyone and forgive quickly.

4) Be slow to judge and do not allow others to bind you by their consciences.

5) Humbly serve all people.

6) Patiently wait for God's judgment.

7) Never give up hope in Christ.

The best way to use Sundays is to gather with those who believe in Christ, exalt God, commune with those who love him, and encourage one another. We can look on Sunday as a drudgery day when we have to force ourselves to attend services. Or we can see it as an opportunity to join others in praising and thanking our creator, confessing our weaknesses, asking forgiveness and encouraging others.

God bless you and keep you safe!

4

Luke 6:17-26

How To Get Your Heavenly Reward

He went down with them and stood on a level place. A large crowd of his disciples was there and a great number of people from all over Judea, from Jerusalem, and from the coast of Tyre and Sidon, who had come to hear him and to be healed of their diseases. Those troubled by evil spirits were cured, and the people all tried to touch him, because power was coming from him and healing them all.

Looking at his disciples, he said: "Blessed are you who are poor, for yours is the kingdom of God.

Blessed are you who hunger now, for you will be satisfied. Blessed are you who weep now, for you will laugh.

Blessed are you when men hate you, when they exclude you and insult you and reject your name as evil, because of the Son of Man.

Rejoice in that day and leap for joy, because great is your reward in heaven. For that is how their fathers treated the prophets.

But woe to you who are rich, for you have already received your comfort.

Woe to you who are well fed now, for you will go hungry. Woe to you who laugh now, for you will mourn and weep.

Woe to you when all men speak well of you, for that is how their fathers treated the false prophets. (NIV)

Two opposites prevail in life: Blessing-woe. Happiness-misery.

Many become so wretched they want everyone around them to be miserable, too. Most of us swing between happiness and woe.

Based on the current status of your life, where do you feel headed: toward happiness or woe? At points in life, everyone has felt these things Jesus listed: hated, excluded, insulted, rejected, and called evil names.

It is tough being a writer and having publishers reject your manuscript. Having gone through that numerous times, I liken it to asking a girl to be your date for the prom. She says "No." You ask another girl. She says, "Forget it creep!" You keep asking. Some say, "Never! I wouldn't be seen dead with you." You ask every girl in the school. All reject you. Some insult you. That is how it feels to have many editors reject your manuscript.

I went through the same thing earlier in life looking for a job. I have also had people insult me because of my preaching style. I have even been rejected by a group of ministers. I have been an object of racial hatred; been rejected for being white, poor, short, and klutzy. A church leader advised me not to return to a church my wife and I attended for a while. I had not even preached there. I never knew for sure what the problem was; only that the preacher did not approve of me.

Every person becomes an object of insult and rejection at some time or another. Remember the lonely hearts clubs? They have been replaced now by organizations that match you with the perfect mate. Some advertise that they can find exactly the right person for you. The only thing they do not promise is what a rent-a-car company says it will do — "We'll pick you up."

Back to the lonely hearts club. This person sent a picture to the club. They returned it with a note saying, "We're not that lonely!" Sometimes people insult us because we inadvertently do dumb things: A lady was flying with her infant daughter. When they landed, they were met in the waiting area by her granddad, who took the baby while she proceeded to the baggage claim area. Standing there alone waiting to claim her baggage, she was absent-mindedly holding the baby's pacifier. She noticed an airport employee staring at her then at the pacifier, then back at her. Finally the employee spoke. "Excuse me, Miss. Is this your first flight?"

Did you notice how Jesus' advice differs from what most experts give?

Jesus: *Blessed are you when men hate you, when they exclude you and insult you and reject your name as evil.*

The world's experts advise: "If people insult you, reject you, exclude you, hate you and call you bad names, call the proper governmental agency and make sure you get a good attorney to represent you."

The world says: Have you been the victim of discrimination or job harassment? Stand up for your rights. Is the IRS stalking you? Call us. Everyone deserves to be treated right." Jesus took the opposite view. "*Blessed are you when men hate you, when they exclude you and insult you and reject your name as evil ... Rejoice in that day and leap for joy ...*"

Before we jump to conclusions, we need to pay attention to the cause of the rejection and insults — because of the Son of Man. If we are lazy, spiteful, insult others; if we are unfair, dishonest, and difficult, we can expect harassment. We need to straighten up our lives, think of other's needs, and stop blaming other people.

Dr. Wade Ruby was one of my professors at Pepperdine. He used to give what he called "piercing" examinations in the English literature classes I took. Some students complained about their "Ds" and "F's." He gave them little sympathy, simply saying, "That's what you earned." Sometimes we deserve insults for the way we behave. That is why Jesus said in Matthew, *"Settle matters quickly with your adversary who is taking you to court."* On occasion we need people to rebuke us and set us straight.

Here is the kind of rejection Jesus meant: 1) When we suffer because we lovingly try to tell other people about Jesus. Some folks become angry at our attempts to share the good news. They will insult us, not invite us to their parties any more, reject us, and say evil things about us. They are upset because the gospel makes them uncomfortable. Most people just flow downstream in life. Just move along with the crowd. It is comfy doing what the majority does. If you can tread water (dog paddle) you will get along fine. But try going against the current. Gravity works against you as well as the force of the flow.

That is what happens when we change course in life and follow Jesus. It threatens people — silently rebukes their pride. Even church people at times resent the zeal of Jesus' dedicated servants.

"I once had an enemy. He said, 'You are not faithful to our denomination.' Eventually he started to hate me. "At one of the conventions, I went up and said, 'Hello, how are you?' and I hugged him. "He said, 'Don't hug me! I don't love you!' 'I love you, Brother,' I said." 'You cannot love me because I am your enemy.' "I replied", 'Praise the Lord, I know you are my enemy. But this is an opportunity to love my enemy. Thank you, Jesus, for my enemy. Bless you, enemy!' One year later I was preaching in his church. Love is the most powerful' weapon we have."[10]

2) Sometimes the gospel does not reach other people's hearts. We continue to love even though they do not respond. Even when they exclude us, insult us and reject us for Jesus' name.

Acts 3 told of Peter and John seeing a lame man in the temple court of Jerusalem. He was born a cripple. Someone carried him to the temple every day so he could ask people for money. His only means of livelihood was to beg from people as they went to worship at the temple. For forty years, he never walked, and never thought he would. His begging location was an ideal place. It might compare to being at an intersection where the Church of Christ, Methodist, Baptist, and Lutheran churches each had a building.

As Peter and John approached him, the lame man asked them for money. Let me fill you in on a secret. If you want to raise money, do not put preachers at the top of your prospect list. Many of them are skinflints. More than a few live Sunday to Sunday. Peter and John were broke, too. Instead Peter and John both looked at the guy on the ground. His legs had never stretched and straightened. He had never stood upright.

Peter said something odd to the guy, "Look at us." The panhandler did, hoping that they would toss him several shekels. Peter's first word must have depressed the beggar. "We don't have any money." What he heard next probably sounded strange, "What we have, we give you." Still sounds crazy, doesn't it? Peter went on:

10   *Call To Discipleship*, Juan Carlos Ortiz p. 131

"In the name of Jesus Christ of Nazareth, walk." Peter took the guy by the right hand and "helped him up. In an instant the man's feet and ankles became strong."

Dr. Robert Nichols practiced orthopedic surgery and for many years attended the Hollywood church. Dr. Nichols established a crippled children's clinic in Calexico, CA, right across the border from Mexicali. The good doctor assisted thousands of crippled Mexican children. The Hollywood church collected clothing, donated money for braces and casts, and the young people annually held Christmas parties for the children. Norma made hundreds of dolls that brought smiles to little girls and boys. Church people also contributed toys and candy to the kids. Some children suffered the effects of polio. Many were born with club feet. Their feet and ankles were turned so that they could not walk. Some could move only by scooting along the ground. It usually took a series of surgeries over a period of months (sometimes years) to cure their difficulties.

The man Peter and John met was immediately healed. "He jumped to his feet and began to walk. He went with them into the temple courts, walking, leaping, and praising God." People came running from everywhere. They all knew the fellow. They had seen him around town for years. Now he was springing around praising God. Peter said to them, "Why are you amazed?" The power to do this came from the very guy you crucified not long ago. God raised him on the third day and now it is by faith in his name that this poor cripple was healed.

You probably did this in ignorance, but it is something God through his prophets foretold would happen

— that his Christ would suffer. God now commands you to repent if you expect good things to happen to you.

You would expect everyone to be thrilled with what happened. Not all were happy, though. Soon the religious leaders showed up and they were ticked. They did not want Peter and John preaching about the resurrection of Jesus. They cared little that a cripple had been healed; even though he had not walked for forty years.

The leaders tossed the two apostles into jail as though they were common criminals. They did not even charge them with a crime. At a hearing the next day, they asked Peter and John, "By what power or name did you do this?" Those authorities were the same ones who called for Jesus' crucifixion. "It is by the name of Jesus Christ of Nazareth, whom you crucified but whom God raised from the dead," Peter boldly said. The leaders faced a quandary. They knew a miracle took place. The facts were irrefutable. They knew that if the apostles kept preaching about Jesus they would lose their cushy jobs. So they threatened Peter and John.

The two apostles went back to the other believers. They all prayed for more boldness to speak about Jesus — not that the leaders would back off, not that God would perform a miracle to deliver them. They simply asked for more courage to speak the truth about Jesus. They performed additional miracles and brought many to Jesus. Out of jealousy, the officials arrested the apostles and jailed them again. The Lord let them out of jail and told them to get back to preaching. The Lord did not even say to take a couple of days off. "When the sun comes up, it is back to work, fellows."

Someone went to the leaders and told them, "You know the guys you jailed last night? They are out there preaching again." The leaders were steamed. They brought the apostles in. The high priest (the honcho) said "We gave you strict orders not to preach in this name!" He and the other leaders were so furious they wanted to execute the apostles. A rabbi who had been Paul's mentor told them not to be so rash. So they ordered that the apostles be flogged — laid stripes on their backs using a whip that had ends of bone and metal. They demanded that they not preach anymore in the name of Jesus.

In a remarkable verse, Acts 5:41, *"the apostles left the Sanhedrin, rejoicing because they had been counted worthy of suffering disgrace for the name."* Verse 42 reads: *"Day after day, in the temple courts and from house to house, they never stopped teaching and proclaiming the good news that Jesus is the Christ."*

I pray that we shall all prepare to do that and rejoice if we are called to suffer on behalf of his name. That's what Christians are called to do.

Brother Yun, a Chinese Christian, related his experiences: "For months we lived like hunted animals, never knowing where we would sleep at night or when we might be hauled away by the authorities. "The government and the Three-Self Patriotic Movement have fooled many Christians around the world by insisting there is freedom of religion in China, freedom for people to choose. They boldly claim Christians are no longer persecuted for their faith. "My own personal experiences — as well as those of thousands of other house church believers — are quite the opposite. On one occasion when I was arrested the authorities let me choose whether I wanted to be shocked with an electric baton or whipped with a rope. They mocked me and said, "This is your free choice."

"There is freedom of religion in China only if you're willing to do, say, live, and worship exactly as the government instructs you. Anyone who desires to live a godly life and obey all of Jesus' teachings will soon find out how much freedom there really is."[11]

Jesus said, "If you suffer persecution, rejection, and insults for my name, be happy, you will receive a heavenly reward."

I pray that we are all ready.

Our days of persecution might be at hand.

God bless you as you remain faithful in your trials!

---

11 *The Heavenly Man: the remarkable true story of Chinese Christian Brother Yun*, p – 70

5
Luke 6:37-38

Are You Using The Right Measuring Cups?

Do not judge, and you will not be judged. Do not condemn and you will not be condemned. Forgive, and you will be forgiven.

Give and it will be given to you. A good measure, pressed down, shaken together and running over will be poured into your lap. For with the measure you use, it will be measured to you. (NIV)

Do you get nervous, when you hear a preacher mention the word "give"? Does it make you think it's time to check your wallet or purse? "I knew it would happen someday," you are thinking, "and now just before Thanksgiving, the preacher thinks I should give more." It occurs in many churches. Nearly every tenth sermon urges us to tithe or to give more.

Two men were shipwrecked on a desert island. One was a churchgoer and the other was not. The minute they arrived on the island, the non-churchgoer began screaming and yelling, "We're going to die! There's no food! No water! We're going to die!" The church-go-er calmly propped himself against a palm tree and it drove the other guy crazy. "Don't you understand? We're going to die! What's wrong with you?" "You don't understand," said the churchgoer, "I make one hundred thousand dollars a week." "What difference does that make?" asked the non-churchgoer. "We're on a desert island. We're going to die." The churchgoer smiled, "You just don't get it. I make one hundred thousand dollars a week, and I tithe. My minister will find me!"

I cannot remember speaking on the subject of money in the seventeen years I have preached here. It does not seem necessary. You are generous in other ways so your giving probably reflects it. If people are walking right, they do not need lectures about staying on the path. I have no idea what any of you gives; and I don't want to know. It is better I don't. But this text mentions giving: *Give and it will be given to you. A good measure, pressed down, shaken together and running over will be poured into your lap. For with the measure you use, it will be measured to you.* You heard the word "give." In his Sermon on the Mount Jesus said, *"Lay up for yourselves treasures in heaven."*

When a Bible text says: *"Give and it will be given to you,"* what else can one talk about? I read about a stingy man who died and somehow went to heaven. He was met at the front gate by an angel, who led him on a tour of houses on the golden streets. They passed mansion after beautiful mansion until they came to the end of a street on the outskirts, then stopped in front of a tiny shack that had no gold paving in front. "And here is where you will be living, sir," the angel announced. "Me live here?" the stingy man yelled. "How come?" The angel replied, "I did the best I could with the money you sent us." [12] If you are not big-hearted in your giving, you might have a problem.

Our question today is: When Jesus said, *"Give and it will be given to you,"* was he talking dollars, shekels, pounds, or Euros? It is doubtful this text has to do

12   The two above stories are found in *World's Greatest collection of Church Jokes,* Compiled and edited by Paul M. Miller

with giving money, at least not directly. Money does not appear to be Jesus' main subject. But if Jesus was not talking about giving money, what was he talking about? Jesus was the world's best ever communicator. He knew how to help people visualize ideas. That is why he told so many parables or stories.

Our text is not a parable or story; still it creates good visual pictures. We like the thought of getting a little extra for our money. Do you know whatever happened to the "baker's dozen," thirteen for the price of twelve? You rarely hear that expression anymore. Our daughter tells me that a Southern California bagel chain still features thirteen bagels for the price of twelve and calls it a baker's dozen. Now and then you see a package label that reads something like: "20% extra for free." The idea of getting additional product for the same price appeals to us, doesn't it?

I read about a butcher who learned to make happier customers by doing the following: If someone ordered a pound of hamburger, he always put less than a pound on the scales the first time and then added to it rather than put more than a pound on and then take away from it. It left a positive image in the buyer's mind. Jesus was talking about that kind of transaction — that type of deal. All buyers love that picture. *"A good measure, pressed down, shaken together, running over."* I love to research the origins of terms. That led me to investigate the words in this text. It took more time than I planned because in the original, these are not garden variety words.

One point of explanation; these are not the words Jesus used that day. Jesus probably spoke Aramaic and

Luke wrote his gospel in Greek. I do not doubt a minute, though, that Luke accurately conveyed what Jesus originally taught. With that explanation let's go on.

A brief look at Luke's terms sharpens the picture for us: There is one term Luke used that you will recognize — the word "measure." In the original, it is the word from which we get metric and meter. While in this country we still use feet, inches, cups, quarts and gallons, much of the world uses the metric system. We are getting there though; we drink liters of many liquids — in fact, many liters of many kinds of liquids.

The word meter simply means measure. Your water meter measures the amount of water you drink, wash and bathe with, and flush every month. The word translated measure is the word meter in the original.

What kind of measure are we considering? First is the word translated "good;" it refers to an abundance. So the Lord begins with this abundant measure and then "presses it down." One source I consulted said the word "press" meant, "Press with the foot." I cannot confirm the accuracy of the source, but stepping or stomping on things usually compacts them, doesn't it? There is also some evidence that the word "press" was used to describe crushing olives.[13] In Jesus' time they evidently did not crush olives the way Lucille Ball stomped grapes in her famous TV scene.

In Jesus' day, they pressed olives with heavy stones. Either way, the image of compressing to get more contents into the container is clear. You start with a good amount, and compress it really well — as you would try to force something into a US Mail Flat Rate box. Next, you shake it. We are not talking a gentle shake as you would test a fragile Christmas package.

13 The Greek Septuagint Version translated Micah 6:15 using the same word for press as in Luke 6:38.

Here's a fascinating fact about the word for "shake" that Luke used. It is often used of shaking of the heavens. You recall those storms that begin with tremendous thunderclaps that rock your house and knock you from your easy chair. You start with a good amount, press it down, shake it hard, and keep adding till it is running over. Luke's term "running over" is descriptive, too. The word begins with the same term that is "hyper" in English. Imagine your sink drain plugged, and water going full force onto the floor — that is hyper-style running over. But note this important detail.

Jesus was not talking about something being wasted. Jesus was speaking about being rewarded with a precious commodity. It started as a full measure, then was pressed down with force, shaken really well, and now is overflowing like the kids' bath water when you leave them to themselves. It is not trickling gently over the edges. Isn't this fun?

Now comes a slight blip on the screen. You need packaging for this precious overflowing commodity. What is the container? The NIV reads: It *"will be poured into your lap."* Rarely do good things pour into our laps. True? Many of us have held little babies and felt surprised by a warm liquid feeling seeping into our laps.

My wife possibly recalls the hot summer day when we and our kids took another couple to Santa Monica Beach. The couple sat in the rear seat, with Peggy the wife, seated behind me. I stopped at a store to buy a bag of ice. As I returned with the cold stuff, Peggy sat with the window open. One of those "rare" mischievous thoughts overflowed my brain. I threw the bag of ice through the open window into her lap. The bag broke.

Not much of the ice stayed in her lap. I think I bought another bag. [14] Few laps hold much of any commodity. After talking about a young woman's lap, I almost hate to tell you how the KJV reads, but in fairness I must. It reads, "Give into your bosom." My wife is probably thinking, it is time for me to stop imagining." So I shall.

So where do we go from here? The word translated "lap" has a wide range of meanings. We should probably best understand it the following way, however: As you know, most people in Jesus' day wore robes. Often a person might pull up the outer robe part way and place commodities in the fold of the garment. For them it was like having a super-sized grocery sack. You get the picture. Give and it will be given to you. A good measure, pressed down, shaken together and running over will be poured into your lap.

A question: what commodity are we discussing here? What is it that is being measured in abundance, pressed down, shaken, and running over? The other day, I read that the Storm Lake, Iowa, city council was proposing to close many of the railroad grade crossings within the city. There have been numerous traffic accidents at those crossings — some fatal. As important as that decision is, the point of today's text is even more vital.

We began by saying that the main point of this text is not your money. That is not the commodity of concern. It can involve money, but that is not Jesus' main subject. So what is the point? Jesus had been talking about dealing with other people — especially enemies and people that might be hard to get along with. People like that are scarce these days, aren't they?

14   Both Peggy and Bart, her husband, thought the incident humorous.

On the subject of dealing with difficult people, let me start with a truth many preachers either do not see or do not want tell you. Jesus was not speaking here about how governments should deal with criminals and law-breakers. Governments are established by God to keep the peace and protect their citizens. When governments punish law-breakers, they do it to protect citizens and maintain civil order; they are not doing it for vengeance, or at least, should not penalize for those reasons. That is what Romans 13 and 1 Peter 2 are about. When governments do not incarcerate and punish criminals, anarchy results.

In our text, Jesus was not referring to the way governments deal with law-breakers. Neither was Jesus referring to the way parents discipline their children. Jesus referred to the personal relationships we have with one another and with our enemies. Our concern as Christians is: How do we deal with unloving people?

In the verses just before our text, Jesus clearly stated:

- If someone hits you on one cheek, turn the other...
- Love your enemies, do good to them...
- Be merciful, just as your father in heaven is merciful.
- Do not judge.
- Do not condemn.
- And forgive others.

That includes not judging or condemning, but forgiving neighbors, family, politicians of the other party, and even ISIS.

Remember, we are not speaking of a government's treatment of those who are guilty of criminal behavior.

The issue is the responsibility of Christians to love and forgive everyone; not judge them or condemn them. We tend to judge and condemn others for the actions they have taken. We get out our tape measures (our standards of behavior), we judge what they have done, and we condemn them on the basis of the rules we set. We do this when they do not measure up to our expectations. We feel good about it because we think we have gotten our measuring principles out of the Bible. The big problem is, the Bible instructs us not to condemn or judge other people.

As Paul reminded the people of Rome, *"It is written, 'It is mine to avenge. I will repay,' says the Lord."* On the contrary: *"if your enemy is hungry, feed him; if he is thirsty, give him something to drink. In doing this you will heap burning coals on his head,"* (Romans 12:19, 20). In our text, Jesus tells us that if we judge and condemn people using the short rulers or yardsticks of human knowledge, God will use those same measuring sticks to judge us. *"With whatever measure you use, it will be measured to you,"* said Jesus. His warning is important: With whatever measure of judging or condemnation we use on others, God will use that same measure on us.

We are to withhold judgment and not condemn. The Lord expects us to be "quick to hear, slow to speak, and slow to get angry" as Jesus' half-brother James advised. If we follow those principles, God will abundantly reward us. In other words, cut others some slack, do not judge or condemn them; forgive others and God will forgive you.

The Lord willing, we shall deal more concerning this subject in a sermon on "listening." Let me close with two scriptures on this principle: First: *"If anyone considers himself religious and yet does not keep a tight rein on his tongue, he deceives himself and his religion is worthless,"* (James 1:26). This Thanksgiving before we take our first bite of turkey or even our hors d'oeuvres, let's bite our tongues before we condemn or criticize or judge anyone.

Second: Ask the Lord's help to forgive everyone (even enemies) as Christ forgave us. *"Be kind and compassionate to one another forgiving each other, just as in Christ God forgave you,"* (Ephesians 4:32). "Give" those things and *"It will be given to you. A good measure, pressed down, shaken together and running over will be poured into your lap"* — or maybe fill your garage.

Happy Thanksgiving!

God bless you and your loved ones!

6

Are You A Relative Of Jesus?

Now Jesus' mother and brothers came to see him, but they were not able to get near him because of the crowd. Someone told him, "Your mother and brothers are standing outside, wanting to see you." He replied, "My mother and brothers are those who hear God's word and put it into practice." (NIV)

Does the sermon title seem odd to you? "Being a relative has to do with genes and chromosomes," you say, "How can I be related to Jesus? Besides, he is the Son of God; what kind of question is that?" In the first place, the thought did not originate with me. It is not my idea. Jesus put it forward. Right here in Luke chapter eight.

"Are you a relative of Jesus?" is the ultimate question. More important than your political affiliation. More important than whether you have paid all of your taxes. More important than your medical history. Vastly more important than your family or whom you married. "More important than family?" you ask.

The other evening I was reading a book by Phil Robertson. Robertson and his family currently appear on the reality show "Duck Dynasty." He grew up hunting and fishing. Robertson became wealthy after he began selling duck calls some years ago. Earlier, he lived a wild life of drunkenness and running from responsibility. He changed after he accepted Christ in his late twenties. He and his wife Kay have four sons.

In his book, *Happy, Happy, Happy*, Robertson talked about marriage. At the age of 66, he'd concluded something: "women are strange creatures." He awoke from a nap one day to find Kay, his wife, standing over him. "'Phil, do you love me?' she asked. 'Yeah, of course I do,' I said. 'Well, write it down then,' she said. 'What?' I asked her as I closed my eyes to go back to sleep. 'Write it down,' she said."

Robertson said that he went back to sleep and awoke at four AM. He planned to go duck hunting. In his living room was a piece of paper. A felt pen sat in the middle of it. Recalling his earlier conversation with Kay, he wrote the following on the paper: "Miss Kay: I love you. I always have, and I always will." He had told her that many times but she wanted him to write it. Kay taped the piece of paper to the headboard of their bed.

"Miss Kay was the perfect woman for me," Robertson wrote. "I was sixteen and she was fifteen when we were married. Nowadays some people might frown on people getting married that young, but I knew that if you married a woman when she was fifteen, she would pluck your ducks. If you waited until she was twenty, she would only pick your pockets," he joked. He maintained, though, that there was an element of truth in it.

He advised young men to look "for nice, pretty country" girls who can cook and who carry their Bibles. It doesn't matter if they are ugly. What's important is whether they can cook squirrels and dumplings. Robertson counsels young men to eat six home-cooked meals prepared by the woman they would like to marry. "If her cooking passes the test, then she's passed the first level. Even more important, she has to carry a

Bible and live by it, because that means she'll stay with you."[15] Phil Robertson wrote about life's most important relationship — marriage.

My wife has never plucked a duck for me. I hope she never has to do that. But she has had to listen to my sermons — twice most Sundays. She's heard my jokes countless times. She has dealt with me during insulin reactions, when I am worse than being drunk. That is a lot for any spouse to bear. I do not need anything posted on the headboard of our bed. I appreciate her and love her.

But Jesus said: *"You have another relative more important than your spouse, your parents or your kids."* The way he said it shocked people then. If folks now knew what Jesus really meant, it would rattle them even more. It opposes lots of tradition and long-held theology. But it is true and we need to talk frankly about it.

A third of the way through Luke's gospel, we have this short, mysterious section. *"Now Jesus' mother and brothers came to see him, but they were not able to get near him because of the crowd."* Jesus spent about 33 years on this planet. Other than the events surrounding his birth, we know little about his childhood.

Matthew and Luke told us that Mary and Joseph lived in Nazareth. The gospels tell us nothing of those early years. The one exception is the trip to Jerusalem when Jesus was twelve. There's no other information until Jesus began his ministry at age thirty. We are left with eighteen years of silence concerning what Jesus did. We have only a hint or two about how he spent his time.

15 *Happy, Happy, Happy,* Phil Robertson with Mark Schlabach, Howard Books, 2013, pp. 51-53

Here is one clue. After Jesus began preaching and appointed his followers, Mark told us Jesus went to his hometown. The people of Nazareth had heard about his miracles. They saw the crowds and heard some of his extraordinary teaching. Mark described what happened in Jesus' hometown: He had been gone a few months, maybe a year or so. Now he was back with some disciples and he had become famous for his wisdom and some miracles. He was in his hometown house of worship, where he attended Bible school. Many were amazed. *"Where did this man get these things?" they asked. "What's this wisdom that has been given him, that he even does miracles! Isn't this the carpenter?"* (Mark 6:3 NIV).

In small towns, most people know one another — especially if they go to the same church. People knew shepherds because they tended to talk to themselves and needed extra cologne. They knew preachers, priests, and rabbis because they always looked for free meals and loved to wear long robes. And people tend to know the carpenters, don't they?

They build, repair, and remodel our houses and neighbors' houses. They knew Jesus and they knew his family. *"Isn't this Mary's son and the brother of James, Joseph, Judas and Simon? Aren't his sisters here with us?"* Joseph had probably died by this time. Remember this.[16] But they knew Mary by name. Mary was likely born and reared there. They knew her other sons by name. Jesus' sisters were still in town: *"Aren't his sisters here with us?"*

---

16 A parallel passage in Luke has the worshipers asking if Jesus isn't Joseph's son, whom everyone then presumed was Jesus' father. Though this presents other questions, the point remains that the locals knew Jesus well. See Luke 4:22

It amazes and troubles many Catholics that Jesus had half brothers and sisters by Mary. It should not surprise them if they knew the *Bible* and Catholic history. Catholic leaders did not declare Mary a perpetual virgin until a few hundred years ago. The gospels make it clear that Jesus had brothers and sisters by Mary.

There are two greater mysteries. We have this eighteen-year period. The gospels say little about what Jesus did from twelve to thirty. This much is evident. The townspeople knew Jesus was the local carpenter. They knew his parents and they knew his siblings. He had likely been at their synagogue every sabbath — more regularly than most of us go to worship.

Their questions were:
- "Where did he get this stuff?
- "We never saw this wisdom before."
- "He never did miracles here."
- "How did this suddenly start happening?"

Those are mysteries.

Here is another mystery and it is baffling. Why did his mother and his siblings not believe in him? Why didn't they have full confidence in Jesus? Mark reported the same thing as Luke: *"Then his mother and his brothers came; and standing outside, they sent to him and called him. A crowd was sitting around him; and they said to him, 'Your mother and your brothers and sisters are outside, asking for you'"* (Mark 3:31, 32 NRSV).

Why were his mother and siblings there? They had come to take him home. They thought he had lost his mind — that he was mentally unstable. Jesus was embarrassing them. John 7: says, *"Even his own brothers did not believe in him."* How did Jesus embarrass his family? For one, He was not a typical rabbi. He did not follow traditional religion. Religious groups have a tendency to set rules and establish traditions.

Most churches now pay more attention to traditions than they do the words of Jesus. For every principle Jesus gave, there are about twenty traditions and additional laws. Someone who does not accept it all is considered weird and a troublemaker. What do I mean by tradition?

Let's say that Brian told one of the teens: Be home by midnight. It is a simple command, isn't it? Be home before the clock strikes twelve o'clock. But let's say uncles, aunts, neighbors, teachers advise the teens concerning that simple commandment: Your dad did not mean that literally. In summertime it doesn't get dark until nine. That hardly gives you any freedom at all. In summer you should be able to stay out until one in the morning. If you have at least ten kids with you, you'll have plenty of escorts. Your dad surely must make allowances for that. It undermines parental authority, doesn't it?

The Lord gave simple commands. Traditions make the simple complicated and they confuse those trying to do right. Religious leaders kept changing laws to suit their own wants. They forced others to follow their traditions. Religious leaders still do that. Jesus said *"That is wrong."* He also hung out with people some considered low-brow and low-class. Jesus did that to help those people know God.

Class conscious people often do not want to accept "low class" folks. Because Jesus did not live by traditions, and hung out with socially unacceptable people, he probably embarrassed his family and his Nazareth neighbors. Jesus' family was upset with him and so were the citizens. Here is what he said in Mark 6:4 (NIV): *"Only in his hometown, among his relatives and in his own house is a prophet without honor."*

His mother had enough doubt that she came with Jesus' siblings to bring him home. His brothers clearly did not believe in him. So much for relatives if they lack confidence in you. Luke 8:20: *"Someone told him, 'Your mother and brothers are standing outside, wanting to see you.'"* They had no faith in him. He embarrassed them. *"My mother and brothers are those who hear God's word and put it into practice," Jesus replied."*

Here is the vital question: Are you related to Jesus? It is extremely important. Most of us expect to go to heaven someday. We take it for granted, don't we? When we die, we will flit off to heaven and be with grandma and all the good people. But that is not automatic. It is not guaranteed just because we go to church or call ourselves Christians. Jesus made it plain, didn't he?

First, we hear *his* word. Not what the president says or any politician or even a preacher. Not what TV anchors say or the folks on "Saturday Night Live." Not what any Harvard professor, Princeton Theologian, or MIT physicist says. We follow what Jesus tells us.

Have you read any of his words this week or heard any of what he says? Are you putting what Jesus said into practice? Has it become part of your life? Is it changing your behavior?

Real Christians do not just wear Jesus' name. They walk, talk, and live by what he says. *"My mother and brothers are those who hear God's word and put it into practice."*

God bless you as you follow Jesus!

7
Luke 10: 1-12

When It's Time To Clean Your Feet

After this the Lord appointed 72 others and sent them two by two ahead of him to every town and place where he was about to go. He told them, "The harvest is plentiful, but the workers are few. Ask the Lord of the harvest, therefore, to send out workers into his harvest field. Go! I am sending you out like lambs among wolves. Do not take a purse or bag or sandals; and do not greet anyone on the road. When you enter a house, first say, 'Peace to this house.' If a man of peace is there, your peace will rest on him; if not, it will return to you. Stay in that house, eating and drinking whatever they give you, for the worker deserves his wages. Do not move around from house to house.

"When you enter a town and are welcomed, eat what is set before you. Heal the sick who are there and tell them, 'The kingdom of God is near you.' But when you enter a town and are not welcomed, go into its streets and say, 'Even the dust of your town that sticks to our feet we wipe off against you. Yet be sure of this: The kingdom of God is near.' I tell you, it will be more bearable on that day for Sodom than for that town".
(NIV)

There is a mystery about today's text. Hardly anyone mentions it. No one talks about it. During all my years of preaching and reading I have never heard it explained — at least as it should be. You need to hear about it.

Imagine a world-wide corporation.

- A company with more name recognition than Amazon, CocaCola, and Cadillac combined.

- It has more sales people and agents than Wal-Mart, K-Mart, Sears, J.C. Penney, Target, McDonalds, the major airlines, and the IRS.
- The company has a great product. It is as vital as water.
- Every human needs it on a daily basis.
- No competitor has a product equal to it.

With name recognition, a huge sales force, and natural need of the product, the company should constantly flourish. It should be expanding daily. It should continue growing, but it does not. The question is, "Why not?" This vast, well-known company with a superior product, and a huge sales force: why doesn't it grow?

Imagine working for this immense business. Most of us either work for or *have* worked for someone else. I have spoken before of a summer job I had prior to my junior year of high school. My sister's husband helped me get a job working for a building contractor. The contractor employed a few high school students each summer. Most of the guys had worked prior years and were experienced.

I could hammer and saw a little. My first job was nailing backhand. They were building a wooden soffit on a house. I must have bent lots of nails or my arms wore out. Then they asked me to saw several boards the same length on a table saw. I did not know the old maxim, "Measure twice and cut once." I cut many of those boards too short. That is when the boss decided that I should dig a hole for the septic tank — by myself.

Did you ever spend a week trying to dig a hole for a septic tank in rocky soil? My boss had not heard of anyone taking that long either. I doubt I ever thanked my brother-in-law for taking the heat he must have caught for suggesting they hire me. The worst was still to come.

The next company project was remodeling a grain warehouse the size of a football field. It was located near a ghost town called Shaniko, in Eastern Oregon. A few foremen, several carpenters, and some of us students went to work on that job. Each foreman led a crew of guys. I asked the boss what he wanted me to do. "Go assist one of the crews," he said.

At least four crews were working on different projects. I went from one foreman to another asking how I could help. "I've got plenty of help here," each one said. I got the feeling that no one wanted me. Again I worked on a project by myself — shoveling wheat out of small wooden bins in the warehouse.

What does this story have to do with the big company? You know part of my difficulty. I was an inept dreamer. Part of the problem was, however, the fact that I had no job description. Before you can properly do any job, someone needs to define or outline what the job is — what is expected of you. That is one reason many preachers fail. No one tells them what "in heck" they are supposed to do. And the problem with many churches is "they don't know what in heck" they are supposed to do.

That is why many churches do not grow. Even congregations that increase numerically usually do not grow as they should. Leaders do not understand their job descriptions. Members do not know their job descriptions.

Church buildings dedicated to Christ scatter the planet. They number in the hundreds of thousands, in a hundred plus countries. The church has millions of representatives. The product is a life-necessity. It excels all related products. It enjoys great name recognition.

But relatively few people "buy" the product. In most places, Jesus is not selling well. Why not? Church buildings are everywhere. They advertise a life-giving product. Countless sales agents represent him. But this far-flung operation is sputtering. One big reason: Few comprehend their job descriptions. Not many church-goers have any idea what their tasks require.

The New Testament makes two things clear. First, Jesus knew what God sent him to accomplish. Two, he gave us a specific assignment — what he expects of us. Do you know what God wants you to do? Do you know your job description? Let's look first at Jesus' mission.

Recall the mystery of those eighteen silent years: What was Jesus doing between ages twelve and thirty? He began preaching at age thirty. What did he do until he reached that age? He worked as a carpenter. The Nazareth townsfolk knew that. Consider this detail. When Jesus was twelve, Joseph and Mary went with a bunch of people to Jerusalem. On the way back, they found that Jesus was not with the group. He was not home alone. He was in the big city alone.

You take a trip and lose a twelve-year-old son. Where would you expect to find him? Behind a building smoking? In a video arcade? Out on the curb texting his buddy or his girlfriend? Looking at magazines in a news stand? Skateboarding? Playing ball?

As you know, they discovered Jesus in the temple sitting among some religious experts, *"Listening to them and asking them questions,"* (Luke 2:46). Recall what he told Joseph and Mary when they found him in the temple: *"Didn't you know I had to be in my Father's house?"* He already knew what God expected him to do. He knew his job description and he had a plan for getting it done. At age twelve, Jesus already knew about his task.

Here is what I think Jesus did from age twelve to thirty. He worked as a carpenter to help support the family. But he was also at the "library studying" (actually at the synagogue reading) the Old Testament.

He listened to the rabbis and learned what they thought.

He memorized scripture.

He learned how to use scripture as a defense against Satan's temptations. [17]

He also researched the scriptures to find all of the predictions about the Messiah.

That study was important. He later reviewed those scriptures with the two disciples he joined on the road to Emmaus after his resurrection. He also reminded the eleven surviving apostles: *Everything written about me in the Law of Moses, the Prophets, and the Psalms must be fulfilled.* [18]

When Jesus began preaching, he did not just wander the beach looking for followers. He had a plan. Matthew ten tells us that he chose and trained the Twelve for a ministry in Galilee (Northern Israel). Luke 10 informs us Jesus later chose 72 disciples to cover the whole country. Our text is the job description he gave those six dozen or so followers. He planned for them to travel to all of the towns and places he would later visit. He gave them a specific mission.

17 See Matthew 4

18 Luke 24:13-25, 44-49

Many people wanted to follow Jesus. He was a sensation — very popular. To folks who wanted to follow him, he said: This is not a feel-good trip. It is not for the weak-hearted or half-hearted. Luke 9 tells about a guy who wanted to be a disciple, but wanted to bury his father first. Does Jesus' answer sound cruel to you? *"Let the dead bury their own dead, but you go and proclaim the kingdom of God,"* (Luke 9:60). In those days when people died, survivors buried them the same day. Three to five day days did not elapse before burial as happens now.

This fellow's father had not even died yet. He was not ready to make a full commitment to Jesus. That is where many of us are, isn't it? We do not mind being called Christians; we just do not want to be radical about it.

But what is a Christian? And what is a Christian's job description? The book of Acts says that *"The disciples were called Christians first in Antioch,"* (Acts 11:26).

Christians are disciples of Jesus. The word Christian appears three times in the New Testament. The word disciple is used about 250 times.

What is a disciple? A disciple is someone who follows to learn. Can we call ourselves Christians if we are not following Jesus and learning about him? Only you can answer that question for yourself. Remember that fellow in Luke 9 who wanted to bury his father before he started to follow? Remember what Jesus said to him? *"Let the dead bury their own dead, but you go and proclaim the kingdom of God."*

The New Testament frequently uses the word disciple. It also talks about the kingdom of God. That is another important term. Few people talk about the kingdom, either. Most of the preachers who do mention kingdom misapply the term. The kingdom of God refers to God's rule. Some think it is an area on earth that God will control. They look for Jesus to come back to earth someday, set up his kingdom, and rule the world from Jerusalem for a thousand years. Jesus meant a place where God rules all right. But the place he wants to rule is your heart or mind.

It does not matter whether you live in Jerusalem, Cleveland, Cleghorn, or Mobile, Alabama. Jesus wants you to turn control of your life over to him. Not to a church or a *church leader* but to him. He is the Son of God. He died to forgive you. He was raised from the grave. He is more powerful than death. Because of that, here is what he wants us to do: learn about him, follow him, do things his way; put him in control. What does that mean? It means that we live by his moral standards.

We stop worrying. We do what we can today and leave tomorrow to his care. It means we treat people as we want to be treated. It means that we forgive instead of insisting that we have a right to our bitterness. We also encourage others.

If God controls or rules us this way, we are members of his kingdom. God's kingdom is that near to us. We admit that the creator of the universe knows more about life than we do.

We also understand that he knows something else. Not only does he know tomorrow and our hearts, he holds us accountable. Do you remember what else Jesus told that guy who wanted to bury his father? *"You go and proclaim the kingdom of God."* "Isn't that the preacher's job?" people ask. Sure, but it is the job description for every disciple. Acts tells us that before he became a Christian, Paul persecuted disciples. All the Christians had to leave Jerusalem. *But as they were scattered, they went everywhere preaching the word,* (Acts 8:4).

Disciples are not responsible for whether people accept the word; only for telling it.

Our job description is testifying to people about God's goodness in Christ.

If the hearers do not accept, we wipe the town's dirt off of our shoes and go elsewhere.

Suppose we are not even getting our feet dirty telling others about God's goodness? We should question whether we are really his disciples.

- Disciples listen to Jesus' words.
- They learn Jesus' words.
- They do as Jesus says.
- And as long as the Lord keeps them on earth, they tell others about Jesus.

That is our job description. It is exactly what Jesus told the disciples in the Great Commission: *Go and make disciples of all the nations, baptizing them in the name of the Father, and of the Son and of the Holy Spirit, and teaching them to obey everything I have commanded you. And surely I am with you always to the very end of the age.*

Jesus is near. He is Lord of the universe. We wisely let him rule every part of our lives. We also dedicate ourselves to letting others know about God's love in Christ.

We also dust our feet when folks won't listen.

Jesus' time is valuable.

God bless you as you tell others his good news!

8

When To Stop Asking The Lord For Things

One day Jesus was praying in a certain place. When he finished, one of his disciples said to him, "Lord, teach us to pray, just as John taught his disciples." He said to them, "When you pray, say: 'Father, hallowed be your name, your kingdom come. Give us each day our daily bread. Forgive us our sins, for we also forgive everyone who sins against us. And lead us not into temptation.'"

Then he said to them, "Suppose one of you has a friend, and he goes to him at midnight and says, 'Friend, lend me three loaves of bread, because a friend of mine on a journey has come to me, and I have nothing to set before him.'" "Then the one inside answers, 'Don't bother me. The door is already locked, and my children are with me in bed. I can't get up and give you anything.' I tell you, though he will not get up and give him the bread because he is his friend, yet because of the man's boldness he will get up and give him as much as he needs."

"So I say to you: Ask and it will be given to you; seek and you will find; knock and the door will be opened to you. For everyone who asks receives; he who seeks finds; and to him who knocks, the door will be opened."

I just bought a new computer. It is fast. It has lots of memory. It does a thousand tasks I will never use or need. For instance: When I first opened it, I saw a screen full of advertisements for computer games — actually about two and a half screens full. Nothing I could use for writing sermons or books, just a bunch of games. Thursday evening at bedtime, I opened the computer to check on something. The advertisements for all of those games came on the screen. One of them was an Agatha Christie mystery. The object is to find out who murdered a young woman.

The game has musical accompaniment of the type you expect with a mystery. My wife passed by my office, heard that music, and wondered what in the world I was doing. I had been trying to find clues in the attic and bedroom of the deceased young lady in the mystery. My wife was intrigued for a while. "These games could be addictive," she said. She soon left to do something else. I wasted another twenty minutes or so before I gave up trying to solve the mystery. The computer informed me that I was getting a free trial of the game. If I want to play it further, I have to go online and pay. That probably will not happen.

The abundance of games on computers and the numbers of people playing them says a lot about life, doesn't it? Many people like to play through life. They pray little — except in emergencies.

Prayer connects us with the creator of life, the being who designed and made this complex, vast universe. But instead of connecting with the creator in prayer, we play much of our lives away. I admit that I pray more often when I travel by air. I pray most frequently and intensely during takeoffs and landings. Are you the same? During those times, many read, talk, play games, or wear headsets listening to music. They appear unconcerned, evidently not praying. Are twenty-first-century people different from the folks when Jesus lived? I doubt it. The majority of people might have professed religion then, but it does not sound as if most were very godly.

Here is why I think that: In about 30 AD, Peter warned people to save themselves from their crooked generation. Just as it is today, many people then were corrupt. Even religious people in those times knew little about praying. Today's text tells us that. Jesus was the exception. *One day Jesus was praying in a certain place. When he finished, one of his disciples said to him, "Lord, teach us to pray, just as John taught his disciples"* (Luke 11:1).

- Jesus prayed often.
- He prayed intensely.
- When he came up out of the Jordan River after his baptism, Jesus prayed.
- Before he chose his twelve apostles, he prayed all night.
- He likely prayed through a list of one hundred or more men the night before he picked the twelve apostles.
- The night before his crucifixion, Jesus struggled in prayer.

When Jesus chose the twelve disciples, however, it does not appear that they were men of prayer. They became men of prayer but they did not grow up praying. They heard others pray but they did not know how to pray. They probably felt the need to pray at times: They did not travel in airplanes, but they fished in small boats, often at night. Strong winds came suddenly from nowhere. They worried that their boats would capsize. At times their relatives got sick and were near death. Their children got lost and had mishaps.

In similar times most of us feel a need to pray. The apostles were just like we are. If you feel uncertain about prayer, it helps to know that the disciples felt that way, too. When Jesus called the twelve, they were likely at least college age or older. A few of them were possibly quite a bit older: Matthew had been a successful tax agent. He could have been the eldest, but that is only speculation. The twelve disciples wanted to pray as John the Baptist had taught his followers to pray.

Jesus gave them a beginner's lesson. The model prayer Jesus gave them was simple. The Lord does not want long, repetitious prayers from us. *He said to them, "When you pray, say: "'Father, hallowed be your name, your kingdom come. Give us each day our daily bread. Forgive us our sins, for we also forgive everyone who sins against us. And lead us not into temptation.'"* In English or Greek, that prayer has fewer than forty words.

Do you often hear church prayers that short? Jesus' model prayer was brief. The words were simple. Most were everyday terms. They dealt with concerns we still have. The prayer starts with the word, *"'Father,"* In Greek it is the word "pater," from which we get "paternal," having to do with fathers.

For many people, God is remote and unknowable. In Jesus' time, God seemed distant to folks, too. Addressing the creator as "father" or "Abba," as the Jews would say, was new.

A young minister had a makeshift office in a Sunday school room near the back of the church building. A single light on a cord dangled over his small desk. "One afternoon he sat working on his sermon. He heard a shuffling in the hall. 'Who's there?' he asked. A little voice said, 'Daddy, it's me.' The preacher said, 'What do you want, son? Need some money for an ice cream? Come on in and I'll give you a quarter.' The boy sauntered into the room, climbed up on his daddy's lap and said, 'I don't want nothin. I just want to be close to you.'" The preacher told his congregation a truth we all need: "Real prayer is sometimes not wanting anything except to be in the presence of God." Do you feel that need?

"Hallowed be your name" My wife, our two daughters and I attended the 75th anniversary celebration of the Church of Christ in Hollywood. My wife, Norma, and I spent 28 years in ministry there. We thank God for the opportunity of seeing many old coworkers and friends. We witnessed the vitality and excitement as God's Spirit works in the church there now.

Those in charge of that service thanked us, those who labored with us, and others who served the church in subsequent years. God allows us the honor of working for him a short while. Only he can bring real growth to his church, however. We can plant seeds of various kinds and water them. Only God can make the seed of his word grow.

Glory and honor belong to him. He is unique — all powerful, all knowing, and eternal. Only he is like that. That makes him special and holy: *"Father, hallowed be your name."*

Then Jesus prayed, *"your kingdom come."* Roughly translated that means: Dear God, may you soon intervene and straighten out this mess that we have made in the world. May everyone submit to you. May we all allow you and your word to dominate us and our decisions.

While political and religious leaders blame and point fingers at one another, hardly anyone urges us to change our ways and turn back to God. "Repent" is a seriously neglected word. Yet it is the first word Jesus spoke when he began his ministry.

"Give us each day our daily bread." Not many of us are satisfied with daily needs. Not even a thirty day supply satisfies most of us, does it? We want lifetime security. Things resolved permanently — once for all. Politicians and business people promise those things and never deliver. God never promises that in this life. Why not? One reason is he knows that when we feel too secure, we get lazy and proud. But there it is: *"Give us each day our daily bread."*

Now comes the really hard test in the Lord's Prayer, class 101: *Forgive us our sins, for we also forgive everyone who sins against us.* Jesus told us this more than once: In Mark 11:25 he said, *"And when you stand praying, if you hold anything against anyone, forgive him, so that your Father in heaven may forgive your sins."* These are not my words. They are straight from Jesus.

Many of us think we have guaranteed tickets to heaven. But we will not go to heaven unless our sins are forgiven. And our sins are not forgiven until we have forgiven everyone who has offended us. Sitting or standing here today, can you say that you have forgiven every former friend, co-worker, relative, or enemy who has offended you? Every time I think I have dealt with my bitterness, something re-triggers it. Bitterness activates like heartburn after a chili cook-off.

Some folks love computer games because they gain a false sense of control. They enjoy taking vengeance on the games' on-screen enemies. Mowing them down, obliterating them, or annihilating them, makes their day. Computer games offer temporary escape. But they do no more to solve our bitterness issues than a fifth of whiskey aids an alcoholic. Forgiveness is the only effective way to deal with enemies. A morsel of contaminated lettuce can be lethal. So can bits of bitterness.

(4) *Forgive us our sins, for we also forgive everyone who sins against us.*

Another day, Lord willing, we can deal with the line, *lead us not into temptation.* Just this in closing: Jesus wants us to pray for our needs. He wants us to keep asking, seeking, and knocking to obtain them.

I once read about an occurrence during the late 1800s in East Tennessee. There was a famous moonshiner known as Big Haley. Big Haley's real name was Mahala Mullins. Her nickname was appropriate because Big Haley weighed about 500 pounds.

Big Haley and her sons ran a reliable moonshine operation. Their whiskey was renowned. They didn't dilute it and they dealt "honestly." That fact coupled with the problems of arresting a mountain based clan led most of the local law enforcement people to leave Big Haley and her sons alone.

A newly elected sheriff tried to make a name for himself. He prepared an arrest warrant and took it to the judge. The judge signed it but with a scornful smile on his face. He told the sheriff, "Be sure you bring her in."

The new sheriff and his deputies found Mahala's mountain cabin. He knocked on the door, then went in and told Big Haley that she was under arrest. He discovered, however, that Mahala was bigger than the cabin door. After considerable effort, he decided to "unarrest" her. He later told the judge that Big Haley "was catchable, but not fetchable."

Does God answer our prayers? His answers are "fetchable." But we must see that only he can give us the answers. And he gives them only if:

- We stop trying to escape into play and other forms of denial.
- Change our ways.
- Look to him.
- Forgive one another.

Jesus advised us to keep asking, keep seeking and keep knocking. The door will open.

For everyone who asks receives; he who seeks finds; and to him who knocks, the door will be opened.

Our loving creator father is always there. He wants to help you. Just ask him.

Right now.

God bless you!

9

Luke 12:22-31

Dealing With Holiday Worries

Then Jesus said to his disciples: "Therefore I tell you, do not worry about your life, what you will eat; or about your body, what you will wear. Life is more than food, and the body more than clothes. Consider the ravens: They do not sow or reap, they have no storeroom or barn; yet God feeds them. And how much more valuable you are than birds! Who of you by worrying can add a single hour to his life? Since you cannot do this very little thing, why do you worry about the rest? Consider how the lilies grow. They do not labor or spin. Yet I tell you, not even Solomon in all his splendor was dressed like one of these. If that is how God clothes the grass of the field, which is here today, and tomorrow is thrown into the fire, how much more will he clothe you, O you of little faith! And do not set your heart on what you will eat or drink; do not worry about it. For the pagan world runs after all such things, and your Father knows that you need them. But seek his kingdom, and these things will be given to you as well.

Suppose pollsters asked one thousand people to list the worst sins humans can commit. Which sins would you expect to find in the top ten? Jesus covered about ten subjects in his Sermon on the Mount — the longest of his sermons recorded in the New Testament. The topic he gave the most attention in that sermon would not appear in most "top-ten" lists. Few preachers would rank it very high.

You might find these facts interesting: In the Sermon on the Mount, Jesus spent less time talking about murder and adultery than he did this sin. He even spent less time speaking on loving our enemies and giving to the needy than he did this sin. The only subject that appeared to come close to receiving equal time was prayer. You do not have to tell me whether you included it in your list. "You haven't told us what this sin is, Bob," you remark. "How can we say whether it was on our lists?" In case you have not yet guessed, I refer to worrying. How many people of the people you know consider worry a major sin?

Did you hear about the mother who was worried about her son going to church?

She called him on Sunday morning to make sure he got out of bed and was ready for church. "I'm not going," he replied. "Yes, you are going, so get out of that bed!" his mother demanded. "Give me one good reason why I should go," said her son. "I'll give you three good reasons. One, I'm your mother, and I say you're going. Two, you're forty years old, so you're old enough to know better. And three, you're the minister, so you need to be there."

Suppose someone computed the daytime hours Americans spend worrying and the nighttime hours we toss and turn pounding the pillows in our beds. Do you think that number might exceed the number of dollars in the national debt? Jesus told us not to worry about certain things: *"Therefore I tell you, do not worry about your life, what you will eat; or about your body, what you will wear."*

The other evening, I re-read Genesis chapter three on how Adam and Eve sewed fig leaves together to make their first clothes. Remember how they thought they needed some cover after they ate the forbidden fruit? I imagine Eve looking at Adam in his first fig leaf suit saying, "Adam, I don't think that shade of green looks good on you." Then Eve eyed her first dress and asked, "Adam, Do you think these fig leaves make me look short?"

We spend days and nights worrying. Christmas season seems to multiply our worries. Burdens get even worse.

The poor country parson was livid when he confronted his wife with the receipt for a $500 dress she had bought for the Christmas Eve service. "How could you do this?" he exclaimed. "I don't know," she wailed, "I was standing in the store looking at the dress. Then I found myself trying it on. It was like the devil whispered to me, 'Wow, you look great in that dress. You should buy it.'"

"Well," the husband persisted, "you know how to deal with the devil. Just tell him, 'Get behind me, Satan!'" "I did," replied his wife, "but then he said, 'It looks great from back there, too!'"[19]

A few days ago, my wife and I spoke to a young mother who was trying to make the cost of her children's gifts come out even. She was worried about spending the same amount for each of them. Someone else was concerned about spending equal time with in-laws. Many folks will really worry about spending when their bills come due in January. You might share these holiday type worries. But are you also thinking, "What's wrong with worrying? Shouldn't we be concerned about our lives?"

The word for worry basically means "to care." It's a given in life that we'll be concerned about ourselves.

---

19 This story and the one mother-son story were adapted from *The World's Greatest Collection of Church Jokes*.

There is nothing wrong with that. And we need certain basics. Jesus expects us to work and to care for our families. Still, Jesus said many times: "Don't worry." So how can we act responsibly and quit worrying?

Do you recall the thousand people we were going to poll while ago? Suppose that group represents a cross-section of the world's population. Suppose also you could give them a life test. You confine them in an area 150 miles long and 150 miles wide. They must live, work, and die in this contained, controlled area. You place ample resources in the area for them to develop. There is plenty for everyone there. It is up to this group to figure out what to do.

Your purpose in all this is to test them as a group, but also individually. How will they treat one another? How will they use the resources? Will they work and cooperate with others? Will a few band together and control the rest? Will the strong help the weak? Will some hoard and build up resources far beyond what they could ever use? Will some of them form subgroups that exclude others? Remember, this is a test. Will the people in this test area serve, assist, and help one another as you would like to see happen? Or will they think only of themselves?

Life is a test similar to what I have described. The Bible tells us that. Jesus taught that truth. Unless we see that truth, we shall always be fearful, anxious, and worried — if not angry and bitter.

Bible parables, stories, and life histories teach us that we are on trial here. The well-known parables of the sower and the talents illustrate it. Jesus kept saying, "Don't worry about accruing stuff. You won't be staying here long. This is a testing place under God's control." Jesus repeatedly told how God gives us all

BLT tests. Unless you are a strict Jew, you have probably eaten a few BLT sandwiches. I do not often eat them, but they are one of my favorite sandwiches.

But this BLT test has little to do with sandwiches.

The "B" stands for believe in God. The "L" stands for love — love and act in a loving manner. The "T" stands for trusting God.

There is a difference between believing God and trusting God. We usually don't make that distinction, do we? Did you catch what Jesus said about trusting God?

He was speaking to believers when he said: (24) *Consider the ravens* (he did not mean the NFL Baltimore Ravens): *They do not sow or reap, they have no storeroom or barn; yet God feeds them. And how much more valuable you are than birds!* He meant: "Quit worrying about tomorrow!"

Did you take this test into consideration the last time you tossed and turned in your bed worrying about the future? Or worried about what you are going to wear or how long you are going to live? Do you really trust your future to God?

Most of us believe in God and it is beautiful to love; but trusting God to take care of tomorrow is different. We like assurances, guarantees, and peace of mind. The chief goal of many is to avoid pain and stress and to have plenty of money. We want to be happy, to succeed, and live the good life. It gives us peace of mind to eat well and to have our cabinets, closets, and bank accounts full … to enjoy the almost endless selection and variety of foods on store shelves and in restaurants. In this country, most of us eat plenty. We have the waistlines to prove it. Sometimes BLTs are part of the problem, especially if we go heavy on the mayo. We work hard, compete hard, scramble to get ahead and "beat the system," as we like to say.

The world measures success by wealth, power, accomplishments, and fame achieved. You will not take one of those things with you. None of these things matters after you take your last breath. That is what the rich guy learned in the story that preceded today's text. He died suddenly; Jesus comment was: *"Who will get all the possessions this guy prepared? This is how it will be for anyone who stores up things for himself, but is not rich toward God."* (Luke 12:13-21) The rich fellow flunked his test.

Unless we see the big picture, what Jesus tells us will probably not make much sense. God tests us for maturity, sincerity, love for others, honesty, purity, thankfulness toward him, and trust. Are you rich toward God? Jesus kept trying to show us that we are involved in a cosmic battle. There is an element of truth in films and books about wars and evil forces in outer space.

A huge battle is going on throughout the universe. The war between God and evil, God and selfishness; God and human pride. Unless we realize that this battle is taking place, it is hard to understand anything. Life will frustrate and confuse us.

Think of the conflict within you. You are being pulled in different directions. As you know, the battle is this: "Do you fully trust God? Are you confident that if you do what says, he will take care of you?" Unless we can correctly identify the opposing forces in this battle, we will spend a lot of time worrying, frustrated, angry, and anxious. Not many people understand this. We keep trusting the wrong people; trying to impress the wrong people, and we end up disappointed.

God has already won the battle through his Christ-Messiah. When he was on earth, Jesus won the battle against selfishness, greed, impurity, hate, and even death. We need only to believe in him, love as he loved, and faithfully follow him.

One day in 1959 or 1960, while I was a student at Pepperdine, I was working in a new, large, Los Angeles service station at the corner of Wilshire and Crenshaw. The eldest son of the world's richest men pulled up to one of the pumps. He was driving a new Mercedes-Benz hardtop convertible. Probably in his mid-thirties at the time, the son was likeable, congenial, nice looking, very bright, and a family man. His office was across Wilshire Boulevard in the world headquarters of one of Southern California biggest companies.

The service station was the company's flagship station. He was the company president. The son asked me many questions about the operation of the station and I did my best to answer them. Today I cannot tell you any of the questions or any of my answers. However, I can tell you this detail. I was eager to take off my jacket, because I wanted him to see the inscription on the uniform that identified me as the assistant manager of a "most important station" across from the world headquarters of a large oil company, owned by the world's richest man.

You need to know the rest of the story. About a dozen years after that, near the age of fifty, the son died unexpectedly. Hardly anyone now over fifty has heard of that company. The impressive six story building was sold and I doubt any of the thousands of people who will drive by it today has heard of that company or could identify his billionaire father. My greatest regret in respect to the incident is that I did not tell the son of the world's richest man how good God is. I certainly had the opportunity. It wasn't because God hadn't shown me many times. I was just too busy trying to impress an influential man that day.

I was clearly worried about the wrong things at the time; I still get caught up in it often. That day I failed my "pop quiz" or whatever you would like to call it. I pray we shall all recall the BLT, *believe* God; *love* others, always treating them lovingly; and *trust* God in all situations. Only he knows tomorrow.

Today's "Call to Worship" contained these lines from Proverbs 3: *Beloved, preserve sound judgment and discernment, do not let them out of your sight; they will be life for you, an ornament to grace your neck. Then you will go on your way in safety, and your foot will not stumble; when you lie down, you will not be afraid; when you lie down, your sleep will be sweet.*

When we know that God created the universe and that he clearly showed his love and concern for us in Christ, we have nothing to fear. As the apostle John wrote, *"He that is in you is greater than he that is in the world"* (1 John 4:4).

Merry Christmas and happy holidays to you all. May you not worry.

God bless you as you love him and trust him.

10
Luke 12:35-40

Are You A Blessed Slave?

"Be dressed ready for service and keep your lamps burning, like men waiting for their master to return from a wedding banquet, so that when he comes and knocks they can immediately open the door for him. It will be good for those servants whose master finds them watching when he comes. I tell you the truth, he will dress himself to serve, will have them recline at the table and will come and wait on them. It will be good for those servants whose master finds them ready, even if he comes in the second or third watch of the night.

But understand this: If the owner of the house had known at what hour the thief was coming, he would not have let his house be broken into. You also must be ready, because the Son of Man will come at an hour when you do not expect him." (NIV)

Does the question in today's title sound inappropriate? How can any slave be blessed or happy? To people whose ancestors were slaves, the question might seem cruel. So why ask the question? Slavery was common in the first century. It was more ingrained in society than our texting and cell phones. It was almost as ordinary as cars, trucks, and motorcycles. But it did not carry the racial and social implications it does now. Slaves came from all colors and ethnic groups.

Roman laws about slavery were also not the same as in the law of Moses. There were important distinctions between Roman and Old Testament law. The Romans considered a slave no different from a farmer's plow or a cooking pot. He or she was merely an implement with no rights.[20] "But in the ancient biblical East," slaves had "various rights ... these included ownership (even of other slaves) and the power to conduct business while they were yet under their master's control."[21] They were servants with rights and responsibilities. They were people, not things that the rich could use and then dispose at their whims.

Jesus' society was Jewish, but the Romans controlled the world. Both kinds of slavery were seen then. Jesus' listeners saw slavery and some experienced it first-hand. That's why Jesus used human bondage to illustrate truth. Today the subject of slavery creates passion, but we cannot let emotions close our eyes to God's truth in scripture.

My emotions sometimes take over when I try to deal with a new computer — or even an old one. *I get so angry that I stop being reasonable.* Computers work on a system of logic that's built into them. Unfortunately the computers lodged in our craniums are subject to fits of emotion. That is where I often am — in front of my computer having a hissy. Folks say that we need to do things with passion. When I get upset, I have lots of passion. But I am hard to live with and my reason goes "south." Ask my wife. Anger and bitterness disable reason from working to our benefit. Exodus 23:2 advised, *"Don't follow the crowd in doing wrong."* It is easy to get caught up in a crowd's emotions. Taking control of our emotions helps us grasp life's lessons.

In Jesus' time, slavery existed mostly because of economic factors and war. It had less to do with race. So how can his story help us? The servants or slaves in his parable were household workers. Put yourself

20 K.A. Kitchen, *New Bible Dictionary*, p 1195

21 Ibid

in a time and place where people had no cell phones, Blackberries, iPads or PCs. Not that long ago, no one sent emails, text messages, or tweets. The mail could take months. Just last year, that happened to me several times; letters I sent took weeks to reach their destinations.

Here is how limited contact was in Jesus' time. You knew that a visitor was coming only when you heard a bang on your door. That still happens, of course. But it happened regularly then. Many other things were much the same as now. As in the twenty-first century, weddings were big occasions. Jesus was a famous guest at one wedding and even provided the second round of wine (See John 2). Current Iowa weddings are in three parts: First, there is the wedding. Next, the wedding party gets on a bus and goes to an "exciting" town like Remsen[22] for a while. Third is the reception.

There is not total agreement among scholars as to all the customs then. In New Testament times, however, many weddings followed this order:

- **The prearrangement by the parents.**
  When a boy got to 17 or 18, his parents arranged for him to marry a girl about 13-17.
  The girl's parents expected a gift from the groom to offset the bride's loss to them.
  Girls were considered an asset. They cooked, did laundry, and cleaned house.

- **The prearrangement came a year in advance of the wedding ceremony.**

---

22 Remsen is a Northwest Iowa small town known for its many bars. In recent years, just-married couples often rent "party buses" to take the wedding party (bride, groom, male and female attendants) to Remsen where they visit a few of the bars. The bus then delivers the party to the reception. Often the trip to Remsen takes a couple of hours.

The couple was considered legally wed at that time.

If the bride-to-be got pregnant by her husband-to-be, it wasn't considered fornication.

But if she became pregnant by another man, it was adultery.

Remember the dilemma Joseph faced when Mary became pregnant by the Holy Spirit.

Ceremonies were usually held during autumn after the harvest. The nuptials began at the bride's parent's house. Whether they used officiants or what rabbis might have said if they did preside, I do not know. Rabbis resemble preachers and I have personal insight into what they like. They love being seen, heard, and paid.

Weddings probably featured laughter, dancing, eating, and drinking; the latter two, especially by the preachers (rabbis). Guests dressed for the occasion; often hosts provided the fancy clothes. The bride dressed in her embroidered best and she donned jewels. Her attendants gathered round her.

Recall, there was no electricity and windows were rare. So the bridesmaids, "virgins," as they are called in one parable, carried little clay oil lamps. They also swung small vials of lamp oil from cords on their fingers. The vials contained the extra oil those foolish virgins in the parable forgot to bring.

"Meanwhile back at the ranch," the groom and his attendants set out for the wedding. His men carried torches to light the way. On arrival at the bride's house, the bridegroom knocked on the door. When the door was opened, he asked to see his bride. She appeared and her veil was lifted. He gasped with delight as he saw her beautiful face — his new found treasure. At least, that was the hope. And his groomsmen cheered their approval. Do you think that at times there might have been feigned joy by both brides and grooms?

After a banquet at the bride's residence, they set out in joyful procession to the groom's place. Whether they stopped at a town like Remsen, I do not know. If the groom was wealthy, the bride and groom may have been carried in a covered litter. The litter had poles and was lugged by several strong men.

Back at "the ranch," the groom's servants got ready for more celebration. Sometimes events went for a whole week or two weeks. Imagine having to feed, house, and provide booze for that much celebration. You must be wondering where I am going with all of this. We do not have slaves. And it is a rare groom who has not seen most of his bride prior to the marriage. Other parts of the ceremony have changed, except for the expense. Remember, there were no phones and no electric lights. It was also like living in cities now; you kept the door locked because thievery was common.

The first part of the ceremony was at the bride's place. After the celebration and a procession, they left for the groom's house for more partying. The groom's servants or slaves had to be ready. They needed their torches lighted for when that bang on the door came. The servants in waiting had no way to know when the knock might come. It could be a week or two later and it might happen at midnight, two, three, or four in the morning; maybe at sunrise. Whenever, they had to be ready.

They had to be dressed, prepared to serve, with their torches lighted. It is our life lesson, said Jesus. *Be dressed ready for service and keep your lamps burning, like men waiting for their master to return from a wedding banquet, so that when he comes and knocks they can immediately open the door for him.*

We are accountable to God; he is the master of us all. Life is not just about us and our needs. Last week a news story featured a fellow about 30, who lives high: surfing, drinking, looking for girls, eating lobster, and dining well. Lots of guys do this of course.

But he is doing it while on government assistance and living off of others. And he is not even a congressman or President. This fellow has no other stated aim or goal in life. You wonder if he ever wakes up asking why he is here or understanding that he has responsibilities to others.

Most of us are not like this fellow. We work, we help others, and we believe in God. But we still lack the view of life that Jesus taught here. *Be dressed ready for service and keep your lamps burning, like men waiting for their master to return from a wedding banquet, so that when he comes and knocks they can immediately open the door for him.* Are we dressed in a way that glorifies God? Are we ready to serve him other than an hour or two on Sunday? The tough question relates to our readiness for the end. For that bang on the door.

Most of us intend to make a greater commitment to God someday. Just not today. We are not ready for full commitment.

What if you saw the doctor this week and the doc told you that you had only a few hours to live? What would you change? How would you change? What would you say to God? The "bang" on the door can come at any moment. *It will be good for those servants whose master finds them watching when he comes.*

Ever read obituaries? I do not read them every day, and I do not read all of them. What survivors say, I find interesting. Many obituaries are worded: the deceased "died unexpectedly." Because all humans die, no one dies unexpectedly. The time or moment of death often occurs when we do not expect it. But we should all expect to die. Jesus' return will be that way, too. We just do not know the moment of either. That's why Jesus told us to be dressed and ready.

He switched metaphors to emphasize the point: *But understand this: If the owner of the house had known at what hour the thief was coming, he would not have let his house be broken into. You also must be ready, because the Son of Man will come at an hour when you do not expect him."*

Are you dressed and ready, shining with his light?

God bless you as you prepare to meet him!

11

Luke 12: 49-56

When And Where The Lord Doesn't Want Peace

"Shocking and mystifying!" That is what the disciples must have said when they heard Jesus state what is in our text today:

"I have come to bring fire on the earth, and how I wish it were already kindled! But I have a baptism to undergo, and how distressed I am until it is completed! Do you think I came to bring peace on earth? No, I tell you, but division. From now on there will be five in one family divided against each other, three against two and two against three. They will be divided, father against son and son against father, mother against daughter and daughter against mother, mother-in-law against daughter-in-law and daughter-in-law against mother-in-law."

He said to the crowd: "When you see a cloud rising in the west, immediately you say, 'It's going to rain,' and it does. And when the south wind blows, you say, 'It's going to be hot,' and it is. Hypocrites! You know how to interpret the appearance of the earth and the sky. How is it that you don't know how to interpret this present time?" (NIV)

We associate Jesus with peace. The prophet Isaiah foretold that the Christ would be "prince of peace." At his birth, angels announced that that he would bring "peace on earth and goodwill among men." In the sermon on the mount, Jesus said: "Blessed are the peacemakers."

This scripture tells a different story. It is as if Jesus said: *Forget that peace and goodwill stuff. Do you think I came to bring peace on earth? No, I tell you, but division.* Now he is talking fire. Dividing people and setting fires does not sound like something a man of peace does. It is more like what happens during riots in major cities today. How could a "prince of peace" say this? How can a person of peace advise division and casting fire? Are we wrong about Jesus? If so, we follow the wrong leader; we worship the wrong God.

Can we reconcile this seeming contradiction? Understand: there is nothing hidden in the language here. There is not some obscure meaning to any of those words.

The words in the original for peace, divide, and fire meant about the same as ours. Politicians deceive us with tricky language. Jesus did not. He never tried to mislead sincere people. So was Jesus mistaken or forgetful about his peace mission? Why would the prince of peace divide folks and bring fire on the earth?

The answer is related to our earlier question: How can a slave be blessed? Here is the usual thinking: How can there be peace when there is so much injustice? We cannot have peace when people enslave other people. Shouldn't everyone be free? Most of us would like to: Have a peaceful world around us. Live in harmony with our neighbors and our families. End the day and put our head on the pillow in peace, live in freedom, and awaken to peace in the morning.

The question is, "How do you get there?" Few people figure it out. Jesus' contemporaries never did. They

- talked about peace.
- dreamed about peace

- fought for peace
- prayed for peace
- wrote songs about peace
- even preached about peace

They never found peace — never.

For all of their talk and dreams of peace, they never came close. They got misery, war, and hate.

I might have mentioned that when our kids were young, my wife and I hoped to have a peaceful vacation. We took them to Yellowstone Park. For many, it is an ideal vacation spot. The kids did not think so. Other things went wrong. Both she and I were getting frustrated. We were trying to have a good time seeing Old Faithful, the Yellowstone River, the falls, and the bears. The kids kept acting up in the back seat. One of us (I won't say who) leaned over and yelled to the kids: "We're going to enjoy this vacation if we have to beat you to death to do it!"

That sort of thing happened in the first century. They said they wanted peace, talked of peace, dreamed of it, but they did not find either. They literally beat one another to death.

Thank God our kids turned out pretty well despite their sometimes impatient parents — and they bear no physical bruises or marks. We dream of peace — long for it, and pray for it. But it is elusive isn't it? It is like trying to grab a barrel full of eels. We could more easily pick the right multi-million dollar lotto numbers. Why is peace so difficult to find?

We go about it the wrong way. In the first century, they failed, too. Jesus tried to warn his contemporaries. Did you ever watch a loved one about to make a huge mistake? You know what happens. You foresee the misery your loved one is in for. But your loved one won't listen. You try to talk your loved one out of it. If he would just listen, but he does not. I am not being sexist. Just as often that loved one is a she.

During his ministry, Jesus tried to warn his countrymen about their behavior.

- He advised them to love their enemies and pray for them.
- He advised against fomenting insurrection and rebellion against the Roman government and its soldiers.
- He encouraged the Jews to love the Samaritans and vice-versa.
- He advised folks to end their greed, selfishness, and worry, and to live pure lives before God.
- He kept telling his countrymen that their attitudes and behavior had to change.
- They were making a big mistake.

They refused to listen. Hate for Rome increased. So did greed and selfish ambition. As he neared Jerusalem on the day now called Palm Sunday, the man of peace wept, *"If you, even you, had only known on this day what would bring you peace — but now it is hidden from your eyes. The days will come when your enemies will build an embankment against you and encircle you and hem you in on every side ..."* (Luke 19:41-44). Jesus predicted what would happen, and it would not be pretty. Just as Jesus foresaw, the Romans came and destroyed Jerusalem. Women and children suffered horribly.

Here is why many of Jesus' countrymen were upset and angry:

- Foreigners ruled or threatened them
- They paid high taxes

- Politicians were crooked
- There was racial bigotry
- Crime rates were high
- It was not safe to travel by yourself
- Folks locked themselves in at night

If they could just get rid of the foreigners, they could live in peace. Little has changed over two thousand years, has it? Societal challenges weren't the only problem. Personal things frustrated them, also. I'd have peace if: I got rid of this frustrating husband; (had a prettier wife who doesn't nag); had more thoughtful kids; and more generous parents. Had quieter neighbors, lived in a livelier town, and had more money, life would be perfect; I could be at peace.

The answer to peace, they thought, was living in different circumstances. On top of this, they fretted about things that constantly bother us. Life isn't fair.
- Why do some people have more than others?
- Why shouldn't everyone have the same?
- Why do I have to suffer?
- Why should I have it so hard?

Jesus did not deal with inequality issues the way politicians do. Here is the difference: Politicians insist: "Life is not fair, but we are going to make it fair. We know how to fix life's unfairness. We will tax you and fix it." So they take the people's money and create many programs. All guaranteed to work. Few ever do. Most of their efforts worsen the situation.

Jesus agreed that life is not fair. His parables show that he knew its truth. He did not argue the fact. Recall the parable of the guys with different talents? (Luke

19:11-27). One was given ten, another five, and another only one talent. Not everyone is given the same abilities.

Jesus agreed: Life is unfair. Here is why and here is what you do about it. Life is a test. It does not end here. And here is how you get ready. No two people have equal gifts. You have a gift no one else does. Until you are tested, you do not know what you are capable of doing by God's power. That means that we all do our best with what God gives us.

This is where many educators, social scientists, and most politicians get it wrong. When they say they want to make things fair, their goals seem worthy. But no one, especially a politician, can make things fair. First, no one knows the tests God gives. And two, we don't know what anyone is capable of accomplishing. No person knows what she/he can do until the test comes. You know what politicians do. They give a lot of one talent people free tickets in the mail or their bank accounts. And some of those people sit home, watch "The View," gossip on their cell phones, or shop with their EBT cards. Some women become baby factories producing offspring with "fathers" who are out making babies everywhere.

Remember the question the Lord asked the one talent person? "Why didn't you at least do something?" In other words, the Lord says, "I gave you a talent. Why weren't you off of your rear end out there trying to do something with it?" He says to all of us: Keep working. Stop being bitter about injustice. Trust God and forgive. Do things his way. Let God control your life; not bitterness, resentment, greed, or trying to control others.

Are you thinking that Jesus' way will never work? Last week I promised to tell you a true story about a blessed slave. The story also illustrates how to do things God's way. The author Margaret Applegrath related it in her book, *Moment by Moment*.

It is a story of two women and begins prior to World War II. It starts at a seminary in this country. The wives of the professors often met in the quadrangle or courtyard in mid campus. In contrast to many in this country, those professors' wives had it fairly easy, maybe even exhilarating. One of the wives "fell into conversing about her (various) symptoms, until it seemed to everyone within earshot that she would never outgrow a single woe, but merely grow new ones, moment by moment."

Next, the story shifts to China. It begins with Mary Liu's story when she was sold as a slave girl to a "heartless ... young mistress, who used to mistreat the child so viciously that one day she simply tossed her out on a dump heap to die — having already burned both of her feet away. "A missionary ... walking past heard smothered sobbing. She searched for the sound; and found this little mutilated mass of misery. "In the mission hospital they could carve her a pair of wooden feet. But the mangled fingers and palms had to be amputated, with just the unrecognizable remnants of bones left to serve as hands.

"The frightened girl lay on her cot, gloomy and grumbling. But the nurses were gentle. There were dolls, candy, and pictures. There were merry children all over the place. And one day, out of a clear blue sky, Mary Liu became the merriest of all — learning to scamper on small new wooden feet — never for a single moment letting any lack of fingers stop her from doing whatever the others were doing. And always there was sheer joy over each tiny triumph.

"When she finished her schooling, she was made editor of two Christian magazines for Chinese women, *The Messenger* and *The Star*. When the Japanese took over her town, Mary Liu used her wits about preserving her precious stock of paper for the magazines. She had it stacked in dark corners, as if it were worthless stuff, or underneath other piles against the walls as if it were old forgotten numbers, perhaps. "While all the actual trash she stacked pretentiously in careful bundles and treated with such concern that when the inspectors came, it is of course, was what they carted straight out from under her nose, sure that they were hindering and not helping.

"Meanwhile, over in America, the World Day of Prayer committee, which sponsored her magazines through their annual offerings began marveling how Mary Liu seemed able to go on publishing month after month, year after year, when other Chinese enterprises had to stop printing from total lack of paper. Perhaps it was natural, therefore, that when the war was over, Mary Liu should be brought to America to study; and, of course, to be seen! She was always so gay (upbeat) and festive and more sober people fell to wondering just what she found so funny. And especially the seminary professor's wife wondered: 'If I had no feet!' she said to herself, wondering how on earth she would ever get around the quadrangle — she who had two perfectly good feet which had never given her a moment of trouble! Yet here was Mary Liu flitting upstairs and downstairs as fleet as a dancer, and bubbling over with exuberance.

"'If I had no hands!' the professor's wife thought; she who had all her fingers and thumbs, 'How on earth do you do it, my dear?' she was driven to ask. Mary Liu looked her merrily in the eye: 'But see, haven't I everything on earth to be thankful for?' she asked, in surprise and that was the day when the professor's wife started to drop the seven demons which had been possessing her: one by one self-pity and self-love began to be cast out...

"'At least none of you will ever hear me complain again!' she confided to the seminary president, midway of this miracle of being made *'every whit whole'*."[23]

You understand that even if the politicians have good intentions, they are still wrong. We do not know the tests God gives each one. We also do not know what we are capable of doing. We will not know until we put aside our own demons of selfishness, greed, anger, bitterness, and worry and begin trusting God. Should we help others? Yes, without question. We should give generously. But this old maxim is a good one: Never do things for people that they are capable of doing for themselves. Government people do not understand this because of their political motivations, but God's people must.

The apostle Paul gave good advice and served as an example:

> *We work hard with our own hands. When we are cursed, we bless, when we are persecuted, we endure it; when we are slandered, we answer kindly. Up to this moment we have become the scum of the earth, the refuse of the world (1 Corinthians 4:12-13).*

23 *Moment By Moment*, Margaret T. Applegrath, P. 64, 65

Once we follow Jesus as Paul did, we will understand how good God is and what great things he does for those who love him and trust him. Many in the world do not agree with Jesus. He makes them uncomfortable. That is why they make war on believers. That is a great source of division in this world. That is why Jesus' enemies killed him and his followers. We shall never be at peace until we submit to God's way.

Do you think I came to bring peace on earth? No, I tell you, but division.

Jesus' kind of peace and division is the only way.

It is the life I want to follow.

I think you want to follow it, also.

God bless you as you walk with him!

12

Luke 13:22-30

What Door Will You Choose This Year?

*Then Jesus went through the towns and villages, teaching
as he made his way to Jerusalem. Someone asked him, "Lord,
are only a few people going to be saved?" He said to them,
"Make every effort to enter through the narrow door, because
many, I tell you, will try to enter and will not be able to. Once
the owner of the house gets up and closes the door, you will
stand outside knocking and pleading, 'Sir, open the door for
us.'" "But he will answer, 'I don't know you or where you
come from.'"*

*"Then you will say, 'We ate and drank with you, and you
taught in our streets.'" "But he will reply, 'I don't know you
or where you come from. Away from me, all you evildoers!'"*

*"There will be weeping there, and gnashing of teeth, when
you see Abraham, Isaac and Jacob and all the prophets in the
kingdom of God, but you yourselves thrown out. People will
come from east and west and north and south, and will take
their places at the feast in the kingdom of God. Indeed there
are those who are last who will be first, and first who will be
last."* (NIV)

Did you ever arrive at a place you strongly wanted to enter, but you couldn't get in? The door had just
closed. You kicked yourself saying unpleasant things
as you saw your plane pushed away from the gate. At
the concert hall, no one could enter the doors once the
lights were lowered and you missed the performance.

A newly-appointed young minister was contacted
by the local funeral director. The mortician wanted him
to hold a graveside service in a country cemetery. The

deceased had no friends or family left. There was to be no funeral, just that graveside committal. The parson started to the cemetery early enough, but he got lost and he arrived thirty minutes late. He saw no hearse. He saw no funeral director, only some workmen sitting under a tree eating lunch. There was what appeared to be a newly-dug grave. The minister opened his prayer book and read the service over a cement vault. As he returned to his car, one of the workmen said to his co-workers, "Do you think we should tell that parson that he just conducted a service for a septic tank?"

I have never been late when conducting a funeral service. I came embarrassingly close to tardiness, though, for a December 24, funeral in the Los Angeles area. I had to drive about 25 miles in bumper to bumper traffic. The director had already seated the family. One minute before the scheduled hour, I walked through the door — just in time to start the service. I never want that to happen again.

Jesus was not talking about missing a flight, a concert, or a funeral service. In Jesus' story, it is an important banquet — a once in a life-time occasion. Certain folks expect to get through the door when they arrive, but they cannot. The doors are locked and will not re-open — ever.

Here is the sad part. They assumed they would be welcome at the bash. But they were *personae non gratae* — unacceptable at the big party. They never expected anything like this. They thought they were good enough and they figured they knew the host so they could get in whenever they wanted. They banged on the door and identified themselves. But it did no good. It feels awful doesn't it, when someone whom you think should recognize you doesn't?

My second year of college, I attended a small Christian school in Oklahoma. My Greek professor was vice-president of the college. I was in his class nearly every day of the school year. About a dozen students dropped out of that class after the first semester. During the second semester, only three of us were left in class. At the graduation ceremony, the professor surprised me with an award. A few years later, I saw him at Pepperdine in Southern California where he had come to hold a lecture. He did not even recognize me. My ordinarily adequate ego felt as flattened as if a full honey wagon — what farmers often call manure spreaders — had run over it heaving that wonderful stuff all over me.

Something like that happened at the closed-door banquet. Lots of people felt they deserved to sit inside celebrating with VIPs. Instead, the doors closed in their faces. They stood outside insisting the host knew them and that they belonged inside. "Sorry," said the host, "I do not know you."

Jesus clearly spoke of the "Big Shindig." The party before the ship leaves port. All the famous Old Testament guys were feasting, including Abraham, Isaac, Jacob, Moses, David, Elijah, Ruth, Esther, and Huldah. Some folks were there from other countries.

What really amazed the bunch was who had been locked out. Hardly anyone expected that foreigners would be allowed at the banquet. But aliens were inside feasting with the VIPs. And folks, who expected to be there, could not get in the door. Their names had never been on the guest list. "I've never even heard of you," said the host.

Was the host rude? Or did those folks deserve to be left outside? For a fact, most church-goers never hear this parable. I am not sure how many preachers talk about it. To my knowledge, it never appears in the lectionary readings. I have only this observation about it.

A person has various dreams over a lifetime. Two dreams should help illustrate my point. One night about forty years ago, a dream I had was so funny I woke up laughing. My wife was convinced I had lost it. On another night, I had a different sort of dream. It began innocently.

Things were cool. Two angels stopped to tell me that they were looking for someone who was supposed to die that night. Nothing about the messengers in the dream seemed ominous or frightful. It was as though they were simply asking for directions. I spent about four years of my life working in big city service stations and I gave lots of directions to lost people.

The dream went on for some time with a discussion about the identity of the customer-victim they were seeking. I was trying to help them find the right party. After more searching, one of the death angels suddenly pointed at me and said, "You are the one we are looking for. You are the one scheduled to die tonight." I awoke from that dream, too. I did not wake up laughing. My skin color was probably so white my wife could not tell me from the sheets. My heart felt as if a huge-bore diesel engine was pounding in my chest. I expected it to stop with a bang any second. I begged the Lord to help me. It took several seconds for me to calm down.

I prefer that those two angels do not make a repeat appearance. I do not wish them on you, either. But there is a comparison I need to mention. I think the hearts of those guys shut out of the banquet pounded harder than my heart did after my death-angel dream.

It was probably even harder than they had pounded on the door. Those guys spent a lifetime on earth. They were religious and they expected to a have a good seat at the big party. They were not even invited. They were outside looking in. Yet people they considered less worthy were inside celebrating. Those religious leaders, however, were shut out forever.

Could we be making the same mistake they did? Is it possible that we are making wrong assumptions about our religion? Many scholars do not even deal with this parable. They see it only as Luke's variation of a similar parable found in Matthew 7:13-14. It is a separate parable, however, and it refers to a serious matter. It is about what life means and how we should use life.

We often look to scholars and "experts" in the Bible to help us. The same occurred in Jesus' time. The scholars and religious leaders then were messing up big time. They invented laws for people that went far beyond the Lord's original commands.

Imagine driving a road on an important trip. On every highway, some signs and warnings are necessary. But if directional signs are too frequent and too complicated, it is difficult to absorb the information glut, isn't it? When we are overwhelmed with signs, it is hard to concentrate on driving. The laws religious leaders make for others have the same effect. They overload people with directions, exceptions, and fine points of law.

You would do yourself a huge favor if you took a few minutes to read Luke chapters nine through thirteen. In that section, Jesus heavily criticized Jewish leaders for making laws that they themselves did not keep, for parading in long, fancy robes, and for being hypocritical. Current Christian ministers often berate the Jewish scribes and Pharisees for their mistakes. It is clear, though, that Christian leaders are often guilty of doing the same thing.

When Jesus pointed to the mistakes of leaders, they fiercely opposed him. Instead of helping others see and experience God's love, they acted like wild animals. Their behavior showed they were not heaven material (Luke 11:53-54).

The greed of many wealthy people proved that they were not good material either. These two truths confused lots of ordinary folks. The religious guys knew all of this stuff and they were not cutting it. The wealthy folks could afford to give lavish gifts and presumably pile up credits with God. They did not qualify either. A big smelly camel had a better chance of walking through the eye of a sewing needle than the wealthy did of attaining heaven, said Jesus. Thus the question in our text: "Lord, are only a few people going to be saved?"

About 45 years ago, I sat in the office of an old, unbelieving, Los Angeles doctor. He loved throwing scientific "curves" at me. The comment he made that day, however, had nothing to do with science. I had been trying to help an elderly lady, who was one of his patients. He said to me very pointedly about my dealings with her: "Bob, you make grace too cheap." It took me a long time to appreciate what the old physician meant. I think now that many ministers (that includes me) have made grace too cheap.

It is true that Jesus paid the full penalty for our sin. But hear closely what Jesus said about the question of qualifying for heaven: *"Make every effort to enter through the narrow door, because many, I tell you, will try to enter and will not be able to."*

That phrase *"make every effort"* is only one word in the original and you know the word. It is the term from which we get our word "agony." The English word "agony" means: extreme and prolonged suffering. The Greek word differs little in meaning. Jesus meant that getting *"to the door"* requires suffering — sometimes of a prolonged type. The word translated *"narrow"* you probably know, too. It is the word from which we get the term "steno" in stenographer. Do they still use court stenographers? Stenography is a narrow or shortened form of typing — typing in shorthand.

It can take much striving to get to and through that narrow door.

"Once the owner of the house gets up and closes the door, you will stand outside knocking and pleading, 'Sir, open the door for us.'" "But he will answer, 'I don't know you or where you come from.'"

"Then you will say, 'We ate and drank with you, and you taught in our streets.'"

"We went to the dinners where you were and were around when you preached. Don't you remember us?"

"But he will reply, 'I don't know you or where you come from. Away from me, all you evildoers!'"

Both from the text and the context, it sounds to me that Jesus was saying to us:

- If you really know me and want to be with me, you will not act hypocritically.
- You will be the same with your friends as you are at worship.
- You will also claim me as your friend wherever you are.

- You will also assist all other folks in their efforts to find me.
- You will not cause others to stumble.
- You will always act with humility.
- You will always love God, honor God, and praise him.

The apostle Paul wrote two letters to his protégé, Timothy. From all indications, the young preacher struggled mightily with his faith when he preached in Ephesus, one of the worldliest cities of its time:

"Here is a trustworthy saying: If we die with him (Christ) we will also live with him. If we endure, we will also reign with him. If we disown him, he will also disown us (2 Timothy 2:11).

Paul did not promote the idea of cheap grace, either, did he?

Are you striving to enter the door: Jesus, the way, the truth, and the life?

God bless you as you trust him and serve the Lord Jesus Christ!

13
Luke 17:1-4

The Unwanted Necktie Some Might Wear

Jesus said to his disciples: "Things that cause people to sin are bound to come, but woe to that person through whom they come. It would be better for him to be thrown into the sea with a millstone tied around his neck than for him to cause one of these little ones to sin.

"So watch yourselves. If your brother sins, rebuke him, and if he repents, forgive him. If he sins against you seven times in a day, and seven times comes back to you and says, 'I repent,' forgive him." (NIV)

Today's talk is about neckties and pericopes. "What the heck is a pericope?" you say. The word-spell feature on my computer did not know the word "pericope" either. Each time I typed the word pericope, it automatically changed the word to periscope.

If you have watched movies about submarines or have served in the navy, you know what a periscope is. The "peri" part means "around" as in the word perimeter. If you walk the perimeter of your property, you walk all the way around it. The "peri" in periscope refers to around something, and the "scope" part, as you know means "to see." A periscope is a viewing device on a submarine. While the boat is a few feet underwater, the skipper can raise the "the seeing device" and look around.

In pericope "peri" means around, too, but the cope part means to cut. Pericope means to "cut around." You probably hear about three or four pericopes every Sunday, if you are in church, that is. Most scripture readings are pericopes. Though the words have only the letter "s" to differentiate them, pericope is pronounced pe·rick'o·pē. I had trouble finding the correct diacritical mark for "o" in pericope, but this gives you the idea. Accent is on the second syllable and the last "e" is long.

Pericopes are sections of scripture that have been cut around or out (selected) for a particular purpose. You understand the reason church leaders "cut out" or select shorter readings. Few churchgoers come prepared to sit and listen to the whole book of Luke, Deuteronomy, Psalms, or wherever the reading might be found.

Why have I brought up the subject of pericopes? You might like to hear the conclusions some scholars have reached about pericopes. Their suppositions affect how people view Jesus. Here is an example. As you know, each of the four gospels gives a little different perspective of Jesus. For instance Matthew's gospel includes Jesus' Sermon on the Mount (chapters 5-7). The Sermon on the Mount has nine Beatitudes. The first of the nine Beatitudes reads: "Blessed are the poor in Spirit, for theirs is the kingdom of heaven." Luke's gospel contains only four Beatitudes. Just after those four beatitudes in Luke's gospel, Jesus pronounces four "Woes" like, "Woe to you who are rich..." (6:24). Matthew has nine Beatitudes and no woes.

In Luke's gospel, Jesus gave four Beatitudes and four woes. Not only that, Jesus' first Beatitude in Matthew reads: "Blessed are the poor in Spirit, for theirs is the kingdom of heaven." Luke's reads: "Blessed are you who are poor, for yours is the kingdom of God." In

Matthew's version of this Beatitude, Jesus encouraged humility.

In Luke's account, there's a blessing in being poor. Other notable differences occur. Luke wrote that Jesus taught his Beatitudes on a level place; Matthew says that Jesus taught them on a mountain. Scholars carefully cut out or select scriptures like these — lay them side by side and note the differences. These sections they call "pericopes" — the word you now know — if you did not before today.

So why are Matthew and Luke different? What do most scholars conclude after examining these pericopes or scripture sections? Many evidently think that Jesus never said anything more than once. If there are variations, they came about because the gospel writers had different agendas. They assume that Jesus never used an illustration or taught on a subject more than once. If there is a difference in the gospel accounts, which gospel has the original version? Or did any gospel writer state correctly what Jesus said? Many think at least three of the gospel writers used a source scholars refer to as document "Q." These scholars decided that document "Q" contained or was closer to Jesus' real sayings. Though these scholars think "Q" existed, no copies of it have ever been found.

This type of supposition causes many folks to doubt. People question the Bible's reliability and they doubt Jesus. Many of the student-ministers with whom I began college gave up believing for one reason or another. This type of scholarship did not help. If these so-called scholarly approaches did not have such serious consequences, such as happened to many of my fellow students, they would be laughable. You wonder if some reputedly intelligent, well-educated people ever attended the "school" of common sense.

I first began questioning some of this scholarship when I was taking graduate classes at Pepperdine. One class was a seminar on the New Testament book of Acts. I have always been thankful for the professor, Dr. Frank Pack, I admired his scholarship and his strong belief. Dr. Pack was not part of my problem. I wondered, however, about some of the scholars who had written about the book of Acts; their commentaries were part of my reading assignments.

Here is what I mean: the book of Acts describes three mission trips by the apostle Paul. On Paul's first missionary journey, he and Barnabas took Barnabas' young cousin John Mark with them. They sailed from the Mediterranean port of Antioch, spent some time on the island of Cyprus, and then took another ship to a port called Perga in southern Turkey.

The book of Acts tells us that as soon as they got to Turkey, young John Mark decided to go home. We do not know the reason John Mark did; we know only that Paul and Barnabas disagreed on whether to take him on the next mission trip. Scholars speculate: "Why did young John Mark quit the mission trip?"

In the dozens of commentaries on Acts I have read, I have seen many theories. Guesses range from Mark's seasickness, to homesickness, and concern over who should be in charge, Paul or his elder cousin Barnabas. Let me ask you a question. A young man starts on a mission trip and after he is away a while, he wants to go home. What reason would you think is the likeliest?

We shall take a poll, but first let me relate a couple of experiences. Before, I have mentioned that when I was ten years old, my family moved from Kansas to Oregon. While they tried to find a place in Oregon, for about six weeks, the parents left my brother Don and me in San Jose, CA, with relatives. Don and I spent a lot of time together and had fun, but I missed my mom and dad. I also missed my Kansas friends. I was terribly homesick.

Four years later, I was enjoying life in Oregon. I am not sure my parents enjoyed me much at the time so that summer they sent me back to Kansas to stay with my two married sisters. I think my sisters and their husbands got tired of me, too. One sister got me a job working as a farmhand in western Kansas. For weeks I stayed with a young farmer and his wife on a wheat farm miles from town. They hired one other farmhand, an old guy; by old I mean he was at least 45. When you are fourteen, everyone over thirty looks old. I got lonesome on that farm several miles from Scott City, Kansas. I was not homesick for my mom and dad, brothers or sisters, however.

Every day I drove old John Deere and Massey-Harris tractors around endless, hot, dry Kansas fields. As I drove those tractors, I dreamed, I imagined, I yearned to see ... fourteen-year-old Oregon and Kansas girls coming to the field ready to keep me company. I could name some eighty-year-old widower farmers today who dream of a woman (a bit older — I mean older than fourteen of course) with whom they could share company and talk.

Are you ready to take that poll?

- How many of you think it is likely that John Mark was lonesome for his parents?
- How many of you think John Mark got seasick?

- How many of you think that John Mark was upset about leadership on the mission trip?
- How many of you think it is likely that John Mark missed a girl back home?

No scholar I have read suggested the possibility that Mark had a girl friend or possibly a wife back home.

Earlier I mentioned scholars who assume Jesus preached sermons only one time. Let's look at the presumption that Jesus preached sermons or taught parables only once. Has a preacher, professor, teacher, or politician ever existed who did not deliver a speech or lecture more than once? To assume that Jesus used the material in the Sermon on the Mount only one time is as silly as assuming a young man in his twenties never includes a girl in his plans.

Jesus taught in virtually all of the cities and towns in Israel. He spoke to many kinds of audiences. In some instances, children were present. He addressed other presentations to learned scholars. Sometimes speakers use the same story to emphasize different points.

Not long ago, my wife asked me about an illustration I used in a sermon. "Didn't you use that story before?" she wondered. I did use that story, but I told it to illustrate a different point.

In fact not long ago, I mentioned my family's move from Kansas to Oregon, but I used the story to illustrate our need for faith. Suppose someone remembered that Kansas to Oregon story and the way I applied it at that time and made an entry in his/her diary concerning the matter. Suppose also one of you writes in your diary how I applied that Kansas to Oregon story today but you did not know about my earlier reference.

Next imagine that you meet this other person and you compare the stories several years from now. You recall it referring to my desire to have girl-company at fourteen years of age, and the other person writing that I used the Kansas to Oregon story to illustrate the need for faith. Might there might be a discussion about whose story was correct?

If years later, someone reads both diaries, might that person not wonder, "Did one of the diary writers borrow from the other or have the story wrong?" Jesus had to have taught his lessons many times in numerous locations to different audiences. Sometimes he spoke to poor people and at times to well-off, well-educated people.

He always spoke truth, and I think the gospel writers accurately recorded what he said. Jesus no doubt revised his stories depending on his listeners. Good speakers clearly target their audiences. Matthew was an apostle and heard much of what Jesus said firsthand, but Matthew wrote primarily for Jewish readers. Luke wrote for non-Jews and tells us that he consulted lots of witnesses before he wrote his account. That explains why readers see occasional differences in the application of Jesus' stories, teachings, and parables in the gospel writers. Luke very possibly consulted sources who heard Jesus speaking to audiences with differing needs than the ones Matthew recorded. Mark likely did the same.

I am indebted to many scholars for the research they have done and I continue to consult them. But I have a lot more confidence in Matthew's and Luke's accounts, and in Jesus' words, than I do in human opinions, especially when they form those opinions two thousand years after the fact. Scholars are fallible as I have tried to show and so is this preacher.

Let's look at neckties for a few moments. Jesus said to his disciples: *"Things that cause people to sin are bound to come, but woe to that person through whom they come. It would be better for him to be thrown into the sea with a millstone tied around his neck than for him to cause one of these little ones to sin."*

This text illustrates how Matthew and Luke differed over a similar saying of Jesus — *"Cause one of these little ones to sin."* In Matthew 18, children were present and Jesus was clearly warning adults about causing kids to stumble. In Luke 17, Jesus was not talking about children. The setting is entirely different. So who were the little ones? To find out, we need to go back to Luke chapter 15.

Tax collectors and sinners were coming to listen to Jesus. "Sinners" were people who did not live respectably as most of the religious folks expected or sometimes pretended.

Tax collectors were independent contractors who operated as franchisees for the Roman government to assess and collect taxes. (See Zacchaeus , for example, in Luke 19:1-10). They guaranteed the Roman government so much a year and then charged people exorbitant amounts. Tax collectors were notorious cheaters and were usually very wealthy. Despite their backgrounds and behavior, some of these tax collectors and sinful people genuinely wanted to hear what Jesus taught.

In fact, Jesus had "broken bread" with some of them. When these "sinners" appeared in the crowd, the so-called respectable people did not like it. They criticized Jesus for allowing them even to listen. These sinful people wanting to hear what Jesus had to say were "the little ones."

Let's try to view life from the perspective that Jesus taught. We are all needy, lonesome to an extent, and all trying to make our way through life. Jesus came to show us how to get through these lonely deserts of life. None of us has life on our own. No amount of money can buy life. In a sense each of us is by himself or herself.

Our only hope is God in Christ. He came from God. Only he can get us back to God. As the writer of Hebrews urged, *"Let us run with perseverance the race that is set before us looking to Jesus the pioneer and perfecter of our faith ..."* (2:1b, 2a). So we are running and stumbling along trying to get to heaven looking to Jesus, who alone knows the way. The way is difficult. We get distracted, carry demanding loads, and we easily stumble. *"Things that cause people to sin are bound to come,"* said Jesus. You know how hard it is to keep going at times. You wonder if anyone cares, and the world certainly does not encourage you.

Our first obligation is to keep our eyes on Jesus. Our second obligation is to love others and help them get to know Jesus, too. That includes not causing them to stumble and fall — helping them in their struggles with temptation. That is where neckties come into view. In the instance Matthew related, Jesus emphasized the importance of not causing children to stumble. But in Luke's gospel, Jesus shows his concern for folks that some religious people consider unimportant. Tax collectors and sinners for example; the kinds of people church folks often shun. Jesus said, if you cause one of these little ones to stumble, you would be better off having a "cement necktie" and being thrown into the ocean. A millstone would weigh a lot. Not even a Navy Seal would swim to safety with one of those tied around his/her neck.

The word translated "tied around" (verse 17:20) actually contains the prefix "peri," around.

What things cause people to stumble? In Luke 15 and 16, Jesus told two parables that suggest how happy God is when someone changes his/her life and comes back to him.

If you have been out there wandering by yourself, just know that all heaven will be thrilled to have you back in the fold. Next, Jesus told about two brothers. One was the prodigal, who wasted his life and a lot of the family fortune before he realized how much his father loved him. His elder brother was not happy to see him home. He resented his brother and got angry with his father for forgiving his brother. He forgot that if it were not for his father, he would not have anything either.

Jesus summarized several parables and stories in this statement: *"So watch yourselves. If your brother sins, rebuke him, and if he repents, forgive him,"* (v. 17:3). If someone offends you make sure you go to that person and carefully explain the offense. Do not run and tell everyone in town how you have been wronged. Do not send a text message to everyone else in the family or at work. Go to that person first and try to resolve the problem: *"If your brother sins, rebuke him."* Do not involve anyone else until you have attempted to rectify the matter. Do not cause a brother, sister, son, daughter, neighbor, or even an enemy to stumble by refusing to forgive.

That statement *"If your brother sins, rebuke him, and if he repents, forgive him"* is not hard to understand is it? If scholars and we spent more time doing what Jesus said, and less time trying to be critical of the Bible and one another ... there would be a lot less rioting, less looting, less burning, less demanding and marching, less gossiping, tweeting, and texting. Instead we would see a lot more forgiveness and tears of joy. Millions would find peace and love in the Lord.

God bless you as you put your faith in him and as you help others in their struggles along the way.

God bless you as you trust God and lovingly forgive others.

CPSIA information can be obtained
at www.ICGtesting.com
Printed in the USA
FFHW011020091218
49804377-54313FF

9 780788 028953